THE BLUE TARP BIBLE

THE BLUE TARP BIBLE

BEST USES, WORST ABUSES
OF THE (UNSIGHTLY)
FABRIC THAT BINDS AMERICA

RON C. JUDD

SKIPSTONE

Published by Skipstone, an imprint of The Mountaineers Books

Printed in the United States of America

First printing 2008
10 09 08   5 4 3 2 1

Copy Editor: Christine Ummel Hosler
Cover, Design & Layout: Peggy Egerdahl
Illustrations: Christine Cox

ISBN 13: 978-1-59485-089-9

Library of Congress Cataloging-in-Publication Data
Judd, Ron C.
  The blue tarp bible : best uses, worse abuses of the (unsightly) fabric that binds America / Ron C. Judd.
    p. cm.
  ISBN 978-1-59485-089-9 (pb)
  1. Outdoor recreation—Equipment and supplies—Design and construction. 2. Landscape construction—Equipment and supplies—Design and construction. 3. Protective coverings—United states. 4. Implements, utensils, etc.—Materials—United States—Humor. 5. Plastic films—Humor. I. Title.
  GV191.623.J83 2008
  677'.4—dc22

                        200704891

Skipstone books may be purchased for corporate, educational, or other promotional sales. For special discounts and information, contact our Sales Department at 800-553-4453 or mbooks@mountaineersbooks.org.

Skipstone
1001 SW Klickitat Way
Suite 201
Seattle, Washington 98134
206.223.6303
www.skipstonepress.org
www.mountaineersbooks.org

♻ Printed on recycled paper

LIVE LIFE. MAKE RIPPLES.

CONTENTS

Acknowledgments 7

Introduction 8

TARP APPLICATION 1: Dead 1967 Pontiac Le Mans Cover-up . . 18

TARP APPLICATION 2: Kitchen Remodel 20

TARP APPLICATION 3: Windbreak 22

TARP APPLICATION 4: Cover for a Pile of Blue Tarps 25

TARP APPLICATION 5: Dog Sheath 27

TARP APPLICATION 6: Emergency Weekend Kite 30

TARP APPLICATION 7: Emergency Shower Stall 34

TARP APPLICATION 8: Poor Man's — *Really, Really Poor* Man's —
Slip 'n Slide 37

TARP APPLICATION 9: Sort-of-Waterproof, Definitely-
Not-Breathable Rain Poncho 40

TARP APPLICATION 10: Grizzly-Proof Bear Wire Sling 44

TARP APPLICATION 11: Bear Bait 48

TARP APPLICATION 12: (Temporary!) Redneck Drapes 51

TARP APPLICATION 13: Redneck Matching Area Rug 56

TARP APPLICATION 14: Backpack Rain Cover Cover 59

TARP APPLICATION 15: Woodpile Cover 62

TARP APPLICATION 16: Photo/Hunting Blind 65

TARP APPLICATION 17: Roof Patch and/or Entire
Residential Roof 69

TARP APPLICATION 18: Car Window Replacement 74

TARP APPLICATION 19: Wheel-less, Barrow-less
Wheelbarrow 76

TARP APPLICATION 20: Landscaping "Water Feature".........79

TARP APPLICATION 21: Brambles-B-Gon Magic Brush-Removal
Wrapper 82

TARP APPLICATION 22: Blue-Collar Toboggan 86

TARP APPLICATION 23: Tent Ground Cloth.................89

TARP APPLICATION 24: Two-Car Garage...................92

TARP APPLICATION 25: Wall-to-Wall Tarpeting.............95

TARP APPLICATION 26: Duvet Cover 100

TARP APPLICATION 27: Kayak 103

TARP APPLICATION 28: Truck-Bed Liner Liner.............106

TARP APPLICATION 29: Man Purse........................110

TARP APPLICATION 30: Tablecloth 114

TARP APPLICATION 31: Water Cooler.....................116

TARP APPLICATION 32: Weedkiller.......................119

TARP APPLICATION 33: Jed Clampett Rooftop
Carryall...........................121

TARP APPLICATION 34: Five-Minute Rain Fly.............124

TARP APPLICATION 35: Truck Load Cover 127

TARP APPLICATION 36: Sail.............................130

TARP APPLICATION 37: Drag Chute......................133

TARP APPLICATION 38: Industrial-Strength Zipless
Freezer Baggie 135

TARP APPLICATION 39: Unabomber-Style Tarpaper-
Shack Mood Skylight..............138

TARP APPLICATION 40: Low-Budget Pool
Cover/Body Bag..................141

DEDICATION

This book is dedicated to my dad, Ronald L. Judd,
a great man and the best father a young camper
could ever have. At some point, likely in the process
of erecting a windbreak in a gale up above Winthrop,
Washington, Dad accidentally wrapped me in
my first blue tarp — and then taught me the more
priceless skill of laughing at myself as I remained
hopelessly wrapped in them into adulthood.

ACKNOWLEDGMENTS

The author wishes to thank the entire island nation of Great Britain, whose scientists many years ago discovered the wonders of polyethylene, which would later be fashioned into plastic strands, which were woven into sheets, which in turn were coated with more plastic, dyed, and extruded into massive rolls, which then were sliced into individual tarps, which now cover millions of dead 1968 Camaros in backyards all around the globe. A bloody fine contribution to humanity, if you ask us.

Thanks also to MJ, who, miraculously, puts up with this nonsense at home on a daily basis.

INTRODUCTION

FOR BETTER OR WORSE, it's part of the very fabric of our being.

Oh sure, we like to put on airs, talking up our technology, culture, and art, especially when foreigners are listening. But deep down, we know the truth: Americans are the people of the Big Blue Tarp (like deities and other objects of our worship, it merits full capitalization).

There can be no doubt: at this very moment, the venerable Big Blue Tarp is being unfurled somewhere, from one end of the United States to the other.

You'll see one covering the remains of a dinosaur skeleton at a dig in Utah. Holding a body for examination by crime-scene detectives on TV's *CSI*. Creating a Pacific-size ocean of blue by covering up your neighbor's crippled Winnebago in the alleyway.

Big Blue Tarps fly even more frequently in corners of the country cursed by extreme weather. In the Northwest — a wet, triangular corner of the map that for our purposes stretches from Oregon to Alaska to Montana — the Big Blue Tarp is a red badge of courage in a lifelong war against mildew and other moisture-related unpleasantries.

Want proof? Next time you fly into Portland, Sea-Tac, or Anchorage International Airports on that rare, clear day, take a moment to look down.

Blue over there. More blue over there. Big patch of blue down below. Thousands of little ones off in the distance.

In Southern California, you'd be looking at swimming pools. In the Northwest? Acre after acre of tarps.

Big Blue Tarps covering woodpiles. Big Blue Tarps covering '68 Buicks with no hoods. Big Blue Tarps covering entire rooftops. Big Blue Tarps covering stacks of folded Little Blue Tarps.

But this rampant tarpage isn't just limited to the outer extremes of the country. Blue tarps, in fact, can be found just about anywhere there's running water — and in even greater concentrations in places where there's not.

The tarp became a symbol — a none-too-proud one, at that — of devastation and neglect after hurricanes swept through the Gulf States in the past decade. In New Orleans, a city nearly wiped off the map by Hurricane Katrina, Tarp Blue became the local color du jour as the Federal Emergency Management Agency scrambled to make up for a slow start by tacking tacky tarps on residential roofs damaged by the storm — and leaving them there, semipermanently, like a Band-Aid over a wound that just might, if you left it alone long enough, heal itself.

People are still waiting, and some of those blue tarps are still holding.

Southerners, getting in the spirit, have written songs about the tarp (in the "Blue Tarp Blues" genre), installed it on the rooftop of the stable in Christmas nativity scenes, and even worn it as functional clothing in Blue Tarp fashion shows.

Bottom line: The tarp, now more than ever, is woven into the DNA of the land of red, white, and blue. We Americans always know what to do with one, and we'd never know what to do without one. When and where we use them says something—very loudly, in many cases—about just who we are.

Got a problem too big to handle, too expensive to fix, too embarrassing to be seen? Tarp it over, baby. You can come back to it a few years from now, when your mind is fresh. The Big Blue Tarp is a societal Post-it note with a message in block letters: "*Yeah, I know.* I'll get back to this mess later."

And for a lot of us, that's the problem. Big Blue Tarps don't last forever, but they outlast a lot of their unfurlers. Not only do we usually never get back to that original problem, but the problem is so effectively covered by the blue tarp that, more often than not, we forget what the problem was in the first place.

Guilty as charged.

Given all this, it's easy to see how the Big Blue Tarp— available at any good general store, in sizes ranging from 4 feet by 6 feet to 30 feet by 40 feet, and by special order in

I-need-to-cover-my-entire-roof sizes—has come to be one of the first visible signs of urban and suburban decay.

The Big Blue Tarp is a touch of gray hair on the edges of your neighborhood. Who among us has not had the following dinner conversation?

> **HUSBAND:** "Did you see the collapsing shed over at the Martins' place?"
> **WIFE:** "Yeah. They've got a Big Blue Tarp over it now."
> **HUSBAND, SARCASM DRIPPING:** "Isn't that nice?"

Thanks to its positively electric, otherworldly, flaming blue hue, the Big Blue Tarp isn't just something you do to your own property—it's something you do to the whole neighborhood. Go online and look for yourself. Rare is the city council or planning commission meeting anywhere in the country where, at some point, the clerk hasn't had to enter into the minutes a passage like this:

> *Mr. Snodgrass was in—again—today to discuss the blue tarp matter with city officials. He said he has talked to his neighbors, who own the '68 Monte Carlo with no hood, sitting up on blocks, upon which the tarp rests, but the tarp remains. Wants to know what his options are, short of setting the thing on fire. Motion to make blue tarps illegal within city limits was tabled pending further review of council members' own backyards.*

Thus, we wrestle with the big questions of Big Blue Tarp ethics: That RV leak isn't going to be fixed anytime soon, and you know it. But will the neighbors shun you if you just tarp it and leave it? Is a big brown tarp any less obtrusive than a big blue one? And why does a blue tarp in the neighbor's yard look so offensive out your window, but a similar tarp covering your own problems just seems to meld into the landscape?

There are no easy answers. But one thing I do know: the list of practical applications for the tarp is growing.

As a Seattle-area native and a newspaper columnist dealing for many years with matters of the great outdoors—and, in the process, a lot of kitsch—I issued my first ode to the Big Blue Tarp in the mid-1990s, way before the blue tarp was considered cool, in a cheeseball sort of way, by free-spirited types, and even before it began to be publicly reviled by everyone else.

Given the enthusiastic reader response to that piece, Big Blue Tarp lore has since become a go-to staple in my columns—to the point that many readers have appointed me the keeper of the big box of blue tarp trivia. Rarely a month passes without someone sending a note, photo, clipping, or other documentation of a creative new use for the tarp.

They've mailed photos of eagle nests around Puget Sound with the twigs and branches held fast by strands of used blue tarp. Photos of houses in Michigan completely encased, top to bottom, in tarp. Pictures of major archaeological digs in Egypt, with the world's most priceless artifacts bathed in azure light from a protective blue tarp overhead. Tarps on babies. Tarps on dogs.

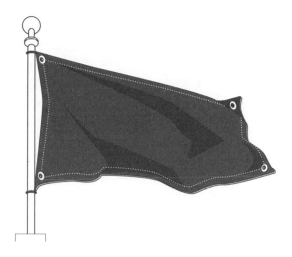

In a world marked by increasing economic, social, religious and political polarization, the blue tarp, quite accidentally and fantastically, has become one of our great common denominators. It has transcended its common usages—of which there are millions—and become a cultural icon, a glaring symbol of our frailty, our indifference, and the side of our nature that veers closest to tackiness.

What's more, the venerable tarp has been offered up, in veins ranging from serious to tongue-in-cheek, as the proposed state flag in Alaska, Oregon, and, more recently, Louisiana, where the sea of blue tarps that sprang up like scabs after the scraping of Katrina remain to this day.

The tarp, in other words, has come an awfully long way for a thin sheet of blue polyethylene glop encasing strands of fibers, churned out by the hundreds of acres for nearly fifty years by giant factories in Asia.

Pieces of it have been to the top of the planet, to the bottom of the ocean, and, we are quite certain, to outer space. The tarp wasn't in the gear chest of the great explorers Burton and Speke in Africa or Lewis and Clark in western America, but only because it hadn't been invented yet. You can bet your life they'd pack some tarps along if they were making similar treks today—and they would sleep drier at night because of it.

In deep woods and high places, the BBT, ingeniously applied, no doubt has even saved lives. In less-inspired uses, it likely has taken a few back.

All the venerable Big Blue Tarp lacks to cement its place in early twenty-first-century American culture is a true homage:

TARPS IN THE NEWS

THE BLUE TARP STATE FLAG

At least three states in the union—Alaska, where the Big Blue Tarp is king and long ago was dubbed the "Alaska flag"; Oregon, aka The Mildew State; and Louisiana, which thanks to hurricanes over the past half-dozen years has been festooned with blue tarps ever since—have seen petitions to make the BBT the official state flag.

A sampling of opinion from residents of all three states turned up only mild support, with one Oregonian and one Alaskan calling a state flag made of blazing tarp blue "redundant" because nearly every household, construction site, and squatter's camp already is flying half a dozen of them anyway.

a partly serious, mostly whimsical love song to the big blue blanket we love to wrap ourselves in.

And that's where this book comes in. It's the full-on ode to the Big Blue Tarp that the nation has been crying out for—well, OK, maybe not *crying out* for, but at least anticipating with subdued excitement. Consider it a heartfelt paean to the grommet-cornered piece of petroleum product nearest to our hearts.

In these pages, you'll find new ways to use the tarps you already own, and you'll discover even more reasons to revile the ones deployed by that certain tacky someone who lives across the street.

To put it simply, this is a celebration of the Big Blue Tarp, long may it wave, flap, drape, or just hang limply over the stern of a boat that'll never again see water. Take a moment, turn the pages, and for once give the blue tarp the respect it deserves.

Yes, it's tacky. Sure, it's cheesy. And undoubtedly, it is Grade A butt ugly.

But that's just the view from the outside. From inside the comforting embrace of a big tarp, the sky is always blue, and the significance, if we're honest with ourselves, is always clear:

We would be a lesser people without it. The blue tarp—love it or loathe it—is part of the social fabric that ties us all together. Or at least covers up our rough spots.

TARP FAQ

HOW ARE BLUE TARPS MADE?

A: IT'S COMPLICATED. The plastic material in tarps, polyethylene, is an oil-based product discovered by the British in the 1930s. It's now the world's most-used plastic; about 60 million tons of it are produced every year, for everything from McDonald's sundae cups to grocery bags to bulletproof vests.

Early poly tarps were a single sheet of extruded polyethylene, which ripped easily. Modern tarps, with a fabric weight typically 2 to 4 ounces per square yard, are made using either thin strips of polyethylene or, less often, nylon (another plastic) cord, woven together in sheets like a blanket. The woven fabric is then dyed, coated on both sides with more liquid polyethylene or vinyl, and baked.

The finished material is then cut to size. A seam is sewn on the outside, and grommets are punched through at regular intervals. There's your tarp—5 to 8 mm thick in most cases, but larger, heavy-duty models made with larger or more tightly woven cord are up to 15 mm thick.

Final step: The blue tarp is folded and—here's the true irony—wrapped in plastic for shipment to your soggy doorstep.

Tarp Applications

Tarp Application 1

DEAD 1967 PONTIAC LE MANS COVER-UP

(or insert your own make/model here)

WHERE:

A highly conspicuous place in your front yard
(where else?)

PHILOSOPHERS will tell you that every person, place, or thing has its own *raison d'être*, a true reason for its existence. For the Big Blue Tarp, this is it. At this very moment, big blue tarps are covering enough dead cars, from Nome to Tuscaloosa, to keep one of those wrecking-yard car compactors busy until 2065.

Look, I know saying this might cause fistfights in the parking lots of numerous small-town cinder-block taverns with gravel parking lots, but so be it: The classic blue-tarp-over-dead-car-in-front-yard application is our beloved BBT's

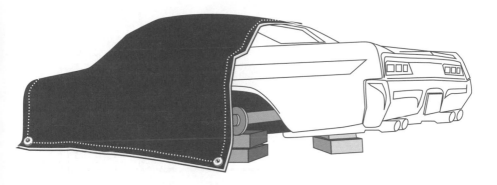

highest calling. If some ghastly decree restricted use of tarps to only one thing, this would have to be it. (Sorry, all you woodpile fans.)

The best thing about putting a tarp over your dead car: It's not just a cover-up, it's a *statement*. Depending on the size of the cajones of its spreader, the tarp over a dead car says the following to neighbors, visiting salesmen, and anyone else passing by:

* "Dead car? What dead car?"
* "Yes, it's a dead car. So sue me. On second thought, give me a month to find a starter motor on eBay.... "
* "Well, sure, it's an eyesore. Wanna try going a few years with the tarp *off?*"
* "Tell it to the hearing examiner. I checked at City Hall and my front yard is definitely zoned Urban Big Blue Tarp/Automotive/Deceased."

Tarp Application 2

WHERE:

Any large dwelling next door that you can see
from every window in your home and every
point outside it

TWO THINGS you can count on as Americans reach middle
age: Guys at some point will attempt an embarrassing comb-
over or ponytail, and women will decide that their avocado-
colored Kenmore dishwasher can no longer be tolerated.

Next thing you know, various disheveled pickup trucks
transporting various ragged contractors will be coming and
going from the family home at all hours—leaving various
blue tarps in their wakes, like slime trails from sun-evading
banana slugs.

You can't really blame the guys in hard hats: This is who

they are and what they do. But you'll have to get used to the fact that many, many blue tarps will be an unfortunate backdrop to your neighborhood life for anywhere from 8 to 1,008 weeks, depending on the number of days that Mr. and Ms. Remodeling Neighbor remain in rehab for Post-Demolition Stress Syndrome. Get used to it.

Important architectural note: If you see a blue tarp fashioned in a funnel shape protruding from the roof of the kitchen remodel-in-progress, it's possible that your neighbor, in an attempt to ward off dehydration and dysentery, is using the tarp to collect rainwater to drink and bathe in while the plumbing contractor searches for his long-lost can of pipe-joint compound. Cut your neighbor a little slack on this: Everything will be up and running in about 44 weeks.

TARP TRIVIA

OOPS: YOUR (BBT) SLIP IS SHOWING

Some eagle-eyed movie viewers discovered a scene in Mel Gibson's 1995 epic *Braveheart* that's of interest to BBT-ophiles. As reported on the Internet Movie Database website: When the English soldier interrupts the wedding, "some sort of box on top of a tripod is visible on the left side, with a blue tarp on it."

Tarp Application 3

WHERE:

Windy campsite/picnic area

YOU REMEMBER camping as a kid, right? Typical sequence:

1 Amid much whining, crashing, yelling, and sometimes bodily harm, the family engages in the joyful activity of packing up the car with provisions for two weeks away from home. (Sample enlightened dialogue: "Has *anyone* seen the wool socks I took camping seven years ago? Well, why not?")

2 Amid much of the same—only with more time to stew over alleged familial transgressions—you unpack the car at the selected campsite, which, no matter where it is on the planet, will smell like mildew.

3 Watch Dad, gear stacked around him in Ringling Brothers-size piles, place a finger to the wind, and, before anything else can commence, utter the seven dreaded words: "We'll need to put up a windbreak!"

4 Dad then commences unfurling a rhinoceros-shaped wad of tattered tarp and a gigantic ball of hopelessly tangled bungee cords, frayed rope, duct tape, and tent poles. Several hours later, sweating but proud, he will stand back and display a flat wall of fabric that to you looks much like one of the original sidewalls of the doomed blimp *Hindenburg*.

5 This observation proves prophetic about 12 seconds later, when a large gust of wind rips the "windbreak" from its moorings and sends it flying into the campfire, after which it continues to sail, like Paul Bunyan's own flaming, demonically possessed ax-polishing rag, all the way through the campground.

Oh, the humanity.

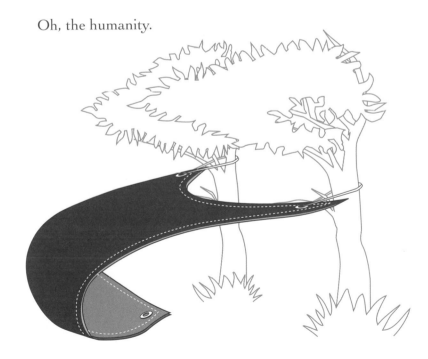

NOTE: A good windbreak should be solidly affixed to trees, an outhouse, an automobile, a medium-size child, or other sturdy object so that, when the wind blows super, super hard, these, too, will be ripped from the ground by their newly affixed drag chute.

ALSO PLEASE NOTE: It's never a good idea to try to erect a windbreak on a really windy day—or any day in which you have already spent many hours undergoing the trauma of loading and unloading the car for a camping trip.

TARPS IN THE NEWS

KEEP THIS NUMBER HANDY

Actual toll-free number, provided by the Corps of Engineers and FEMA, to call when your roof is blown off by a hurricane in the Deep South: 1-888-ROOF-BLU.

Tarp Application 4

COVER FOR A PILE OF BLUE TARPS

WHERE:

Most likely, on the mossy north side
of your house

EVERYBODY needs to have a large pile of big blue tarps somewhere outside the house, ready at a moment's notice to perform some of the admirable chores described herein. But you don't want your unsightly blue tarps just lying around in plain sight. Most common solution: Cover them with an even larger unsightly blue tarp.

Now, we realize that using a blue tarp to cover other blue tarps might seem incestuous in a polyethylene-coated fabric sort of way, and that pondering the ramifications of covering a cover with a cover that hides another cover could cause instant, lasting insanity, like the kind that overtook that guy who wrote himself crazy producing *Zen and the Art of Motorcycle Maintenance*. So don't let your mind go there. Just trust us: One blue tarp out in plain sight beats several dozen others in a pile any day of the week.

In fact, once you have covered your covers, pat yourself on the back, Sparky. By concealing many unsightly tarps with one, you're performing a valuable humanitarian service for all tarp-kind.

TARP FAQ

WHAT'S THE BIGGEST BLUE TARP I CAN BUY?

A: THE SKY'S THE LIMIT, if you're into placing special orders. And a number of U.S. tarp vendors will get you whatever size you need if money is no object. The largest tarps stocked by home-improvement stores are generally 30 feet by 40 feet. If you need one bigger than that, well, maybe you should consider just replacing the whole roof.

Tarp Application 5

DOG SHEATH

WHERE:

Over the body, excepting the head,
of the family pooch

CALL THIS THE HUMANE, anti-conehead approach to
Fido's skin rashes and other common maladies.

You know of what we speak: How many times have you
seen a canine skulking around, humiliated, with one of those
big plastic cones over his head? You might as well tattoo
a label on his mangy hindquarters: "THIS DOG CAN'T STOP
LICKING HIMSELF, SO ARTIFICIAL MEANS HAVE BEEN EMPLOYED."
It's dastardly.

Solution: Any blue tarp owner can turn the tables on this
doggy disgrace by turning the logic on its head: Rather than
keep the pooch's head away from its affected body parts, keep
the affected body parts away from the pooch's head.

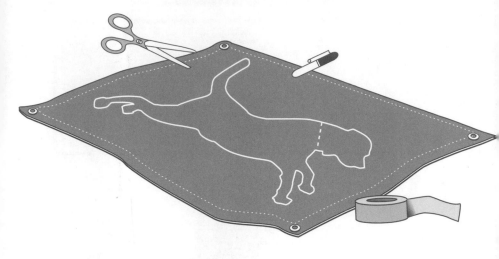

Just follow these simple steps:

1 Make Fido lie on his side on a decent-size blue tarp.
   A 4-by-6-footer should suffice.
2 Trace around him with a Sharpie.
3 Cut out the resulting shape.
4 Create a second dog-shaped cutout by tracing around
   the first cutout.
5 Duct tape the two cutouts together.
6 Cut out a head hole.
7 Install.

Voilà! Rather than suspect your dog of being a lickaholic,
those judgmental neighborhood mutts comprising his peer
group will simply think he's visiting from Ketchikan.

TARPS IN THE NEWS:

WORTH (MORE THAN) THEIR WEIGHT IN GOLD?

Nobody knows for sure exactly how many BBTs were put into action in the wake of hurricanes that devastated much of the U.S. Gulf Coast through the first years of the twenty-first century. But the number surely rates in the millions, as government records show that hundreds of thousands of blue tarps were nailed to roofs as part of the U.S. Corps of Engineers "Operation Blue Roof" in Louisiana alone.

Intrepid reporters called it the most extensive re-roofing job in American history and began to dig up some of the receipts. They expected to encounter a little gouging here and there—the kind you get in emergency situations, where the law of the land is supply and demand. But nothing like what they found.

A Knight-Ridder Newspapers investigation found that "a lack of oversight, generous contracting deals and poor planning mean that government agencies are shelling out as much as 10 times what the temporary fix would normally cost." Contractors were paid an average of $2,480 for less than two hours of work to cover each damaged roof—even though the government provided the tarps for free.

Some roofers conceded that for these "repairs," using blue tarps designed to last three months, what they were paid in some cases exceeded what it would normally cost to *replace the entire roof*.

The fiasco made it all the way to the U.S. Congress, where irritated representatives demanded public hearings to hold roofing contractors and tarp suppliers accountable.

But as far as we know, nobody ever went to jail for the post-hurricane Operation Blue Roof rip-off.

Tarp Application 6

EMERGENCY WEEKEND KITE

WHERE:

Your local park, which, if you live in Omaha, is probably just a fenced-off corner of a wheat field, but if you live somewhere fancy, such as Santa Cruz, might be an aerodynamically correct facility designed especially for kite deployment

IT'S SATURDAY. It's your turn to have Little Kyle.

You pick up Little Kyle, bring him home, and, as usual, place before him a variety of entertainment devices. Lots of options: A basketball. Two mitts and a softball and bat. Swim Fins. Rock 'em Sock 'em Robots. Nintendo Wii. Sony PlayStation. Pay-Per-View. Jenga. Chutes and Ladders. Pinochle. Cribbage. Makita power tools. Four-stage model rocket. iPod.

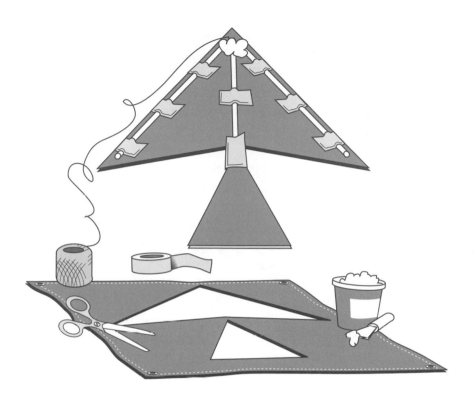

All of which he will survey, sniff loudly, then command: "I WANNA FLY A KITE"

You don't have a kite. You don't know any kite stores. You recall once seeing a kite in Wal-Mart, back before you pledged to never go there again for fear of causing some little Chinese version of Kyle to glue the tops on snow globes for four cents a year.

Then your inner MacGyver kicks in. From the garage you emerge with several lengths of wood dowel, a half roll of duct tape, and your trusty BBT. Seven razor knife cuts later—four on the tarp, three on your thumbs—you produce a stunning, electric-blue delta-winged craft that, although you don't realize it at the time, is constructed of exactly the same materials they're currently using to assemble the all-new, mostly plastic Boeing 787 Dreamliner.

To achieve this parenting triumph, follow these instructions carefully:

1   Cut one large, triangular section from the corner of a Big Blue Tarp of any size. If you can't judge the shape of a kite, distract the kids next door—the kids whose parents are always annoyingly prepared—and borrow theirs for a few minutes, taking it apart piece by piece until you can use it as a pattern.

2   Remove all grommets, old duct tape, snails, or other protruding objects from the cut section of the tarp.

3   Cut a second, smaller triangular section of tarp and duct tape it to the bottom of the first one, so it looks something like a rain slicker for a Stealth bomber.

4   Tape dowels up both sides of the "wing," affixing them at the nose with a lump of plumber's putty or an even larger wad of duct tape.

5   Finally, tie a string to the front and a rag tail to the bottom and take it into the living room, where Little Kyle will be striking out Barry Bonds on Nintendo and will not even look in your general direction.

Oh well. Save your handy Emergency Weekend Kite for another weekend and smile smugly. One distraction in the hand is worth five at the top of a tree. Or something like that.

TARP TRIVIA

BIG BLUE TARPS IN THE ANIMAL KINGDOM

We've seen several instances of wild animals interacting with blue tarps. The most interesting was the recent discovery that large raptors in our area of western Washington have taken to using strips of blue tarp — whether found in strips or torn into strips by the birds, we're not sure — in some of the same ways we do: as a lightweight, waterproof building material for nests. And as we discuss elsewhere, at length, the tarp's value as a bear deterrent/attractant.

But the most fascinating BBT/animal kingdom encounter you're likely to see is at your local horse show. It's true: Trainers some time ago began using blue tarps to train horses. It's all based on a psychology: Horses have an innate fear of unknown objects. Trainers will attempt to eliminate this fear by aversion therapy, if you will — basically making the horses encounter the unknown, thereby learning that it's usually OK.

One common method: Splay out a BBT in front of the horse, then lead him or ride him across it. A lot of horses, seeing the tarp, will naturally decide that, since they have no idea what's under there — 16 feet of water? A gaggle of alligators? Molten lava? — they should just go around. And many will. But with patient repetition, a rider often can coax the horse across the tarp, then eventually get the horse to stand on it without fear.

In other words: You **can** lead a horse to a Big Blue Tarp. It's still unclear whether you can make him drink.

Tarp Application 7

EMERGENCY
SHOWER STALL

WHERE:

An earthquake zone, your local national park, or
any other place where camping is begrudgingly
allowed but shower facilities are harder to come
by than poop bags on sausage-jerky sample
giveaway day at your local dog park

FACE IT: Whether you're in the middle of a three-week
camping trip in Yosemite National Park or fighting to survive
in a post-apocalyptic society where the sun never shines and
Ho Hos are mankind's most valued commodity, sooner or later,
you're going to need to shower. At least if you still want to cozy
up to someone or something anytime in the near future.

Whether your water's coming out of a common garden hose
(for some reason, we still blush whenever we shower with the

one that has "Martha Stewart" stamped on it) or a fancy-pants solar shower (Note: not nearly as effective during nuclear winters), it's best to have a stall to keep prying eyes away.

There are two ways to do this. One: Between trees, buildings, street signs, or other means of support, string rope ties or bungee cords. Hang your tarp from these, like a drape, using bungee cords run through the grommets to secure it. Two: Have your two best friends hold the tarp up around you, and your third best friend pass you the soap.

We personally employed method number one some years ago at a national park that shall go unnamed (Mount Rainier), only to have an overzealous female seasonal ranger catch us in the Act of Cleansing in the First Degree and threaten to throw us out of our campsite in one of the park's finer campgrounds, which also shall go nameless (Ohanapecosh) because, she said, park rules prohibit solar showering, as it pollutes the local dirt.

So, you've been warned. Not everyone takes to the idea of outdoor portable shower stalls. But—and this is confirmed by people who have seen the author naked—erecting one is far preferable to the alternative.

In fact, some outdoorsy types we know have assembled quite fancy outdoor shower rigs, turning PVC plastic pipe into a

frame that can be quickly disassembled when Ranger Betty comes cruising by with her citation pad. All of them employ a Big Blue Tarp as the shower curtain. What else?

It's part and parcel of the outdoor-sudsing experience. There's just something about soaping up with a bottle of Campsuds under the open sky, surrounded by that calming azure-blue tarp hue, that just makes you feel like Mother Nature's son.

Or at least her bastard stepchild.

Tarp Application 8

POOR MAN'S
—*Really, Really Poor Man's*—
SLIP 'N SLIDE

WHERE:

Your backyard

THE COMBINATION of hot days and bored kids calls for desperate measures—like a BBT deployment in your backyard, with a hose left running on top to create a virtual carnival ride only a few feet from the house.

Use it just like you used the official Slip 'n Slide you had when you were a kid. Get a flying start before sliding baseball style on your side or rump onto the wetted tarp, which then (we hope) will send you zipping across from one end to the other. It works better on a hill, of course, and we must offer the following warnings:

* Mole hills, gopher holes, and other major divots beneath the tarp can and will create major raspberries

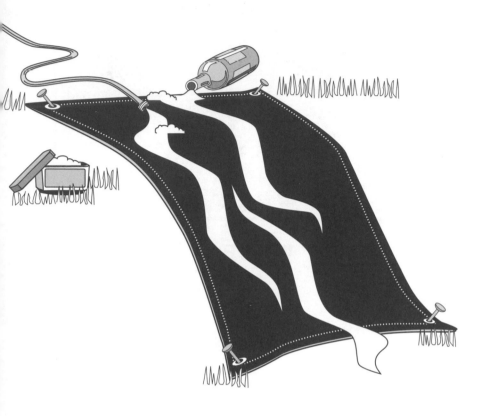

on exposed skin—not to mention scalping the hapless mole or gopher who chooses the worst possible time to stick his head up and have a look around.

* Given the preceding, only the brave and the outright foolish ever attempt to do a Poor Man's Slip 'n Slide face first, à la Pete Rose.
* Petroleum jelly and BBT Slip 'n Slides can be a lethal combination. Whether that's bad or good sort of depends on the crowd.

* The BBT Slip 'n Slide has proven addictive to children in their 20s, 30s, and 40s, particularly if large quantities of adult beverages have been mixed into the water flowing across the BBT. People reportedly have been cited for sliding under the influence in several Midwestern states.

* It is advisable to anchor your BBT to the ground using stakes through the grommets. Otherwise the thing might defy gravity and take off on its own, resulting in a clot of small, wet children and/or inebriated, wet adults moving swiftly downstream through the local municipal drainage system — possibly getting as far as the local metropolitan sewage-treatment facility, where everything unmentionable eventually winds up.

* Slip 'n Sliding can be hard on your lawn. Do it on your neighbor's lawn while he's at work.

TARPS IN THE NEWS

GET THE COLOR RIGHT, PLEASE

Actual correction from the *Arizona Daily Star* of Tucson:

Sept. 5 — A story Saturday on B1 about damage at the Marist College building downtown had the wrong color for the tarps covering an outside corner of the building.

The blue tarps shown in the 2006 file photo were replaced by gray and black tarps nearly a year ago, according to Fred Allison of the Diocese of Tucson.

Tarp Application 9

SORT-OF-WATERPROOF, DEFINITELY-NOT-BREATHABLE RAIN PONCHO

WHERE:

Just about anywhere, except perhaps snooty places, such as Vail, Taos, and lower Manhattan

BEING AN ACTIVE, swarthy outdoorsperson, you will, from time to time, find yourself in need of a protective raincoat that will A) keep you dry and B) not leave you stewing in your own juices like a large quantity of pressure-cooked mutton.

You can—and many of you will—plink down 300 clams or more for a fancy Gore-Tex garment, which, the salesman will tell you, is the only thing available that's truly "waterproof and breathable."

This is partially true. Gore-Tex is, in fact, a wondrous fabric that, judging from its cost, must be made of fibers spun from shredded $1,000 bills. But over the years, we have noted two consistent things about Gore-Tex and its "waterproof/ breathable" kin: It isn't waterproof. And it isn't breathable.

Oh, sure, it'll act waterproof and breathable for a while, provided you don't do something that will void the waterproof/breathable guarantee, such as breathe, move a limb slightly in any direction, stand up, sit down, or blink your eyes. Eventually, water begins to seep in through the seams, and you start to perspire in the thing.

Bottom line: "Breathable" fabric might actually breathe, in the technical sense. But it doesn't *pant*, which is what most of us meaty Americans need in a parka fabric.

This leaves you with only two options: Go ahead and get wet, making sure you have dry stuff to put on before you freeze to death. (You are, after all, covered with skin, the only truly

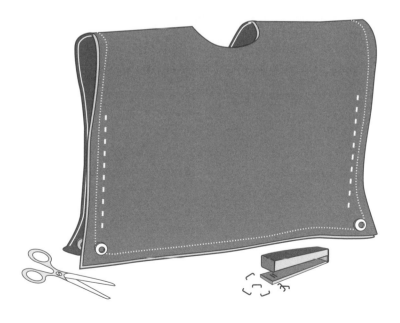

waterproof/breathable substance we know.) Or save yourself a bundle by covering up with something that'll keep the rain off of you, but replace it with equal or greater amounts of sweat. How? Fashion (and we use the term loosely) yourself a classic BBT poncho.

Just follow these easy steps:
1   Acquire one 4-by-6-foot blue tarp, by whatever means necessary.
2   Fold it in half lengthwise.
3   Along the folded top edge, cut a hole for your head.
4   Staple up the sides, leaving holes for your arms—and, if you're smart, armpit breather holes the size of Lake Erie. (BBTs, for all their charm and usefulness, absolutely do not breathe. Never have, never will. C'mon: It'd be just too much to ask.)

NOTE: You'll sweat like a pig in this thing, and you'll look very much like a homeless person. But at least you won't sweat like a pig who just contributed $300 to the Global Gore-Tex "Laughing All the Way to the Bank" Fund. You take your victories where you can get them.

TARPS IN THE NEWS

WHERE DO BIG BLUE TARPS GO WHEN THEY DIE?

The tarping over of much of the U.S. Gulf states caused another problem. Eventually the roofs got fixed—and truly massive quantities of Big Blue Tarps had to be disposed of.

But what does one do with a half acre of blue?

As a Hialeah reader asked the *Miami Herald*'s "Action Line" on November 6, 2006: "Where do all the blue tarps go after being used? Is there a blue tarp heaven?"

The newspaper noted that Habitat for Humanity's local ReStore accepted donated tarps in working condition. But that didn't help those stuck with tarps showing the usual neglect.

Most people wound up throwing them in the trash, which created an all-new debacle.

Garbage workers in many areas complained that tarps mixed with household trash were too big to go through machinery normally used to compact waste. And many tarps wound up wrapped around the working parts of heavy garbage machinery, causing innumerable breakdowns and large repair bills.

No surprise there: Who would expect a BBT, after serving out only a portion of its functional lifespan, to go quietly into the landfill night?

Tarp Application 10

GRIZZLY-PROOF BEAR WIRE SLING

WHERE:

Anyplace you need to keep stuff away from angry bears

NOBODY EVER SAID all this blue tarp advice was going to be clear-cut. So you should know up front that there are two schools of thought on the bear issue—this one and the one in Tarp Application 11. Go with whatever philosophy makes sense to you. (**Humorous side note:** No pressure or anything, but employing the wrong philosophy in the wrong place at the wrong time quite possibly could kill you.)

Imagine this scenario: Once on a trip to Alaska, we were dropped off at a beach camp on the shores of Lake Clark National Park. Glorious spot—not a human soul within 10 miles. And very large brown bear tracks covered 90 percent

of the sand on the beach. Our campsite, at the mouth of a river, was a popular fishing spot for both them and us.

Needless to say, proper bear-awareness techniques were observed. We slept with a large shotgun between us at night, and we made sure everything that had come within 25 feet of food was hoisted up into a tree on a massive bear wire.

Actually, calling our system a "wire" is dishonest. It was more like a heavy-duty block-and-tackle pulley system, with the top end of the cable affixed to the corners of—what else?—a large blue tarp. At night, into the blue tarp went everything from cooking pots to Frosted Flakes to hunting knives—anything that might contain trace smells of food. Up it went, in one glorious, swinging lump, and we slept in relative peace, in spite of the occasional 1,000-pound visitor who gave the camp a good sniffover almost every night.

Make your own facsimile in three easy steps:

1   Put all your cooking gear, food, and anything else that might be mistaken for meat in a large pile.
2   Cover it with a tarp sufficient to enclose the mass.
3   Remove the tarp and lay it flat on the ground. Tie zip cords to the tarp's four corner grommets.
4   Pile all your stuff back on the tarp and hoist it up in a tree, using a pulley or a line thrown over a branch.

The beauty of the system is its holding capacity. Without the catch-all tarp or a similar-size net, you would need so many bear wires that your wilderness camp would start to resemble the trapeze setup for Cirque du Soleil.

In this application, the blue tarp as bear wire sling is wholly effective—assuming you get it way high up a tree. In others? Not so much. Used in other ways, the BBT may not deter bears so successfully. See Tarp Application 11.

TARPS IN THE NEWS

BLUE TARPS CLEARLY VISIBLE FROM SPACE

They really are. Pick a mapping search engine—Google Earth, Wikimapia.org, or the like—and zoom in on your city or town. Sooner or later, you're bound to see blue tarps standing out, in all their glory, like flecks of confetti against the drab landscape.

The big ones, covering large fields for university research, for example, show up first. But in areas covered by high-resolution satellite photography, you can even make out the small tarps covering holes in roofs or decrepit RVs in backyards.

This discovery has been noted by hundreds of intrepid Internet bloggers, including Brian Fitzgerald of Amsterdam, who opined in April 2006:

> *"I HATE Google Earth. I really get lost in it. Seeing places you've been from a heavenly perspective just shouldn't be this addicting, but it is.*
>
> *[But] they've recently upgraded their maps of my adopted home, Amsterdam, and golly, I can actually see the blue tarp roof of my son Doon's fort in the postage-stamp garden in back of our house!"*

It makes you wonder: If there is intelligent life in the universe, what does it think we're hiding?

Tarp Application 11

BEAR BAIT

WHERE:

Anyplace you specifically do *not* want to keep stuff away from bears

AHEM. Although we can personally vouch for the effectiveness of the above-mentioned bear wire/tarp setup—this book, after all, was written on a keyboard by someone with arms, neither of which has been gnawed upon nor off, by a grizzly bear—some caution must be urged.

There is a solid chance that bears didn't bespoil the stuff in that slung blue tarp not because it acted as some sort of effective camouflage but simply because they couldn't reach it, as they sat, staring at it and salivating, from below (adult bears can't climb trees, at least not very high).

Some hunters we know, who have spent many years in the backcountry stalking large game, swear that bears now see blue tarps basically as tablecloths. Reason: So many sloppy hunters and campers have left so much food lying around—

almost always atop, beneath, or somewhere near a Big Blue Tarp—that the bruins automatically associate it with food, the way they would a Coleman cooler or a pic-a-nic basket.

This flies in the face of conventional "wisdom," which holds that bears don't see color well. But people swear it's true.

One of them is Polly Oberosler, a Forest Service wilderness ranger who has spent years patrolling the deep woods of Colorado for junk left by hunters.

"In my travels I have found literally dozens of blue plastic tarps in the wilderness, and they contain all the comforts of home that got left behind, such as toilet seats, tables, jock itch spray, aluminum frame lawn chairs, green fuel bottles, and carpet," she wrote in an article for the *Crested Butte Weekly*.

She noted that tarp blue—a color that does not naturally occur in the woods—seems to draw the attention of bears, which are *not*, in fact, color-blind (another clever myth perpetuated by the Bear Marketing Association).

"They look for blue tarps just as they have looked for picnic baskets and coolers for years," Oberosler writes. "The unopened cans of Dinty Moore stew and fruit cocktail are

invariably among the debris I find as a result of the bear's draw to the blue tarps."

There you have it. You've been warned. That Big Blue Tarp poncho you're proudly wearing into the woods might look like gravy on biscuits to a big, ornery bear. And you thought your rising car insurance rates were something to worry about.

TARP FAQ

HOW LONG WILL A BLUE TARP LAST?

A: PRETTY MUCH FOREVER, if you keep it sealed up in the garage. But out in the real world, where, let's face it, a tarp is most at home, life spans are much shorter. It really depends on where you live: Wind will make a tarp flap and wear thin, or wear through, fairly quickly in spots. But the biggest BBT nemesis—the same for most plastics—is the sun. UV rays will break down the carbon–hydrogen molecules in a BBT's plastic very quickly—in as little as one summer, if you're living in a very sunny place. Roofers who put BBTs on roofs advise customers that the tarps, exposed to constant sun and wind, are usually good for about three months. Your mileage will vary, depending also on the quality of the tarp you begin with.

Tarp Application 12

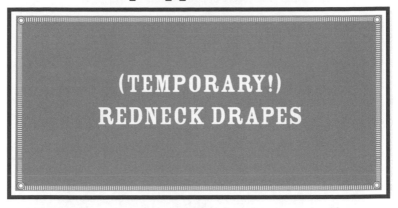

**(TEMPORARY!)
REDNECK DRAPES**

WHERE:

Over your front window, or any other window that most (or better yet, each and every one) of your neighbors must pass at least three times a day

TRUE CONFESSION TIME: A number of years ago, when your humble author bought his first home, the immensity of "home decoration" hit him like a shaving-cream pie in the face.

Nowhere in your basic K–12 education or in the pursuit of the various collegiate degrees thereafter are you sufficiently warned that, once you sign on the dotted line (112 times) to purchase your new home — which will forever after consume roughly 89 percent of your take-home pay — you'll need to fork over another modest 20 grand for basic furnishings.

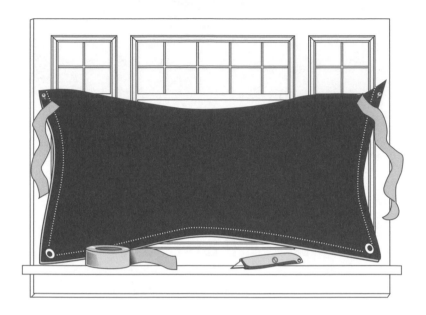

Basic as in *basic*. Like a refrigerator, bar stools, and—this is the killer—window treatments.

It simply had never occurred to me—and a lot of you guys out there will back me up on this, I hope—that windows deserved to be "treated" in any particular way whatsoever. They were just one of those givens in life: You build a house. You put in the windows. You install... blinds, drapes, shutters, something.

Any good American has reason to believe all this is part of the overall package. Back home, growing up, some sort of curtain or blind or somesuch was always there at the ready, covering up the window at night with a mere tug of the cord. But in your brand-new spec house? No, sir.

So you are left with dozens, maybe hundreds of windows—

you never know a house has so many windows until they're all there, bright and blazing away, on the longest day of the year in June. And each and every one of them needs a "treatment" all at once.

Which would be fine, except that even the cheapest "treatment," for even the smallest window, costs more than you'll have for the next 31 years, based on actuarial tables, now that you're a mortgage-paying homeowner. And the complete tab for full-house window coverage one degree above bargain-basement quality is about $5,000.

Now, we already know where you're going here. You're thinking that yours truly, in a fit of the very sort of expediency that led to the unfurling of blue tarps elsewhere in this tome, covered up all the windows in his brand-new house with Big Blue Tarps.

THAT WOULD BE INCORRECT.

But only because, on searching through the 12.7 acres of U-Haul boxes in the garage, I came upon the box containing sheets and beach towels *first*.

I called it a temporary measure. And indeed it was. About a year later, the towels and sheets came down, wood blinds went up—and the birth of a bouncing-baby second mortgage to pay for them was announced by Hallmark card to friends and family.

Do not make the same mistake. Yes, do cover up your windows temporarily, lest your neighbors "get to know" you a lot quicker—and in greater anatomical detail—than either one of you could possibly imagine. But don't use your towels and sheets. Those of you asking "Why not?" clearly have never had the need to dry yourselves with, or sleep upon, a Big Blue Tarp.

NOTE: The gigantic bay window with the sweeping "territorial" view of your neighbor's tarp-covered RV, tarp-covered woodpile, and tarp-covered Irish wolfhound is where your BBT *belongs*. Think of it as sending a message to your new friends: We see your 9-by-12, and raise you a 20-by-30.

So, on to the task. Follow these directions precisely:

1   Lay out a large tarp on the floor in front of the window.
2   Cut the tarp in the approximate shape of the window with a box knife or other object too sharp to take on a U.S. commercial airline flight.
3   Enlisting the aid of a friend or, in a pinch, the person you are sleeping with, boost the tarp up onto the window and tack the upper corners to the wall. (Don't worry about the giant gouges in the plasterboard; these will be covered later by the actual, hoity-toity wall treatments.)
4   Affix a foot-long hunk of duct tape at the tarp's two bottom corners. Leave this hanging loose.
5   Enjoy!

IMPORTANT NOTE: At least once every seven or eight days, remember to go to your window, pull the bottom corners of the tarp up toward the top, and stick the duct tape to the wall, thus "opening your drapes." This will let your neighbors know you are alive and that you might, in fact, be using your new home to live in, rather than to house a large, sophisticated marijuana-growing operation.

Also, it will let light into the room, which is helpful for killing mushrooms and other things growing on the pizza boxes in the corner.

EVEN MORE IMPORTANT NOTE: This is a TEMPORARY TREATMENT ONLY. You owe it to yourself and the rest of the world to take the tarps down and put curtains or blinds up within 48 months—or when the tarp has been hanging for so long that the sun has turned it into loose strips of polyethylene fettuccine. Whichever comes first.

Statute of Tarp Window Treatment Limitations: Nine months.

TARPS IN THE NEWS

TONIGHT ON LARRY KING LIVE—A BLUE TARP IS BOOKED

Actual Larry King transcript from January 13, 2003, from one of a never-ending series of King shows devoted to the tawdry details of the Laci Peterson murder:

LARRY KING: *Dallas, Texas, hello.*

CALLER: *Hi, I just wanted to know what happened to the blue tarp. There was a—if they had a tarp out there at the marina. I want to know if his boat was covered when he went out there with the tarp. I feel like—I just—I feel something. Like he—there's something there."*

KING: *Chief, do we know?*

POLICE CHIEF ROY W. WASDEN: *I couldn't comment on that, but I can tell you that the blue tarp is in our custody, police custody, being examined.*

Tarp Application 13

MATCHING REDNECK AREA RUG

WHERE:

On the floor in front of your (Temporary!)
Redneck Drapes (see Tarp Application 12)

ONCE YOU'RE A HOMEOWNER, you feel it's important
to make things match. At least this is what we recall Martha
Stewart saying one day, back before she went to the hoosegow
for felony abuse of hot glue and pipe cleaners.

And if you've taken the time to decorate your home with
an ingenious—and, need we say it? quite practical—set of
(Temporary!) Redneck Drapes, you're likely to need an area
rug to complement them.

But before we go any further, stop to ask yourself two important questions:

1   Do I have a dog?
2   Do I have/am I planning to have a child?

If the answer to either question is yes, skip this section entirely and proceed directly to Tarp Application 25, Wall-to-Wall Tarpeting.

The rest of you may still need some convincing about the area rug. Well, be honest with yourselves for once: If you've already proven cheeky enough to cover your windows with a Big Blue Tarp, you will, at some point, sit down in front of the plasma bigscreen to enjoy a Hungry Man Dinner during

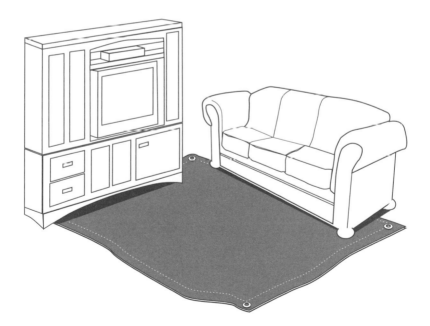

Sunday Night Football. And before the game ends, you will have sprayed chicken bones, bits of macaroni noodles, and several quarts of salsa onto your new carpet.

Not a problem if you have previously installed your Redneck Matching Area Rug, fashioned from a completely unaltered medium-size blue tarp that's been tucked beneath the front of the sofa on one side and beneath the home-entertainment center on the other.

A couple of added benefits beyond the obvious practicality:

*   Ask any furniture expert: Everything goes with neutral tarp blue.
*   Once a month or so, you can pull the tarp up by the corners, drag it outside, shake off the seven or eight pounds of cracker crumbs and — this is our favorite part — literally hose the thing off.*

Decorating Tip: Leaving a Big Blue Tarp on your floor as an area rug for a number of years would be gauche. Change over to a brown one when the mood strikes.

* Special equipment advice for heavy eaters or frequent Taco Bell takeout diners: Pressure washer.

Tarp Application 14

**BACKPACK RAIN
COVER COVER**

WHERE:

On your backpack, over the top of your original
(leaky) rain cover

THE PROBLEM WITH BACKPACKING in a rain forest
is the rain.

This may seem obvious, but if you grow up around a rain
forest—say, in Aberdeen, Washington, or San Juan, Puerto
Rico, where the Olympic and El Junque Rain Forests
(respectively) pelt every encroacher with several hundreds
of inches of rain a year—you eventually start to accept rain
as an imaginary friend that follows you *everywhere*.

And when you're out in the boonies, you adjust accordingly,
taking the extra step of attaching a slip-on nylon rain cover

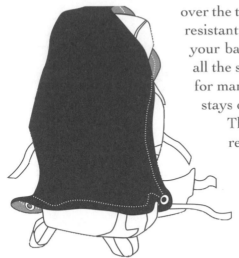

over the top of the existing water-resistant nylon outer coating of your backpack, which contains all the stuff you need to survive for many days—assuming it all stays dry.

There's the rub. "Water-resistant" nylon packs, in our experience, will resist water for about 30 minutes in a good, old-fashioned downpour. At that point, they cry uncle, open all their pores, and let the entire deluge make a beeline for your carefully packed roll of toilet paper and nearby Little Debbie's sponge cakes.

A standard-issue, coated-nylon backpack cover will delay this process by about an hour—or perhaps 10 minutes, depending upon the amount of time you spent sealing its seams before you left home.

SOLUTION: Rain cover cover. When it comes to rainproof layers, the third one usually is the charm. (**Note:** A fourth one might be even better, but let's be realistic: If you apply a rain cover to the rain cover over the rain cover on your water-resistant backpack, someone is going to grab you, pack up your things, and send you away for an extended visit to Camp Obsessive/Compulsive.)

A 4-foot-square piece of tarp—something you should have with you anyway, for any one of the many other uses described here—usually does the trick.

Follow these simple steps:

1   Don't bother trying to shape it to fit neatly over the backpack. Just wrap it all the way around, multiple times, like salami casing. Yes, we know the backpack's shoulder and waist straps are now hidden beneath several layers of tarp. Hold your horses, for God's sake.

2   Exercising care not to slice into the pack body or your own body, slice holes in the tarp for the shoulder and waist straps, and pull them through.

3   Wrap the entire thing with duct tape or bungee cords. Put it back on, and you're good to go.

Yes, you might look like a Sherpa carrying an entire meth lab—or worse—on your back. But this is about comfort, not fashion, remember?

ADDED BONUS: If the weather turns really nasty and you don't have time to pitch your tent, just take the giant blue blob off your back, slice an opening in the front, pull some of the stuff out, and climb inside.

Then look out at the rain, laugh, and think: Just about anyone can survive. But only the wise camper with a rain cover cover will do it with the additional comfort of an entire roll of dry toilet paper.

Tarp Application 15

WOODPILE COVER

WHERE:

Over the top, up the sides, and perhaps even underneath your cord of maple, cherry, birch, fir or what have you

BACK IN THE DAY, when humans traveled by horse, chewed leather, and heated with fire, people probably knew all the firewood basics at an early age. Not us. No, sir.

These days, we only learn the tricks of the trade the hard way, as adults—when, let's face it, nothing comes easy and it takes at least five or six *more* calamities to get a lesson to sink in than it did when we were young tykes.

Then, at some point in our development, we find ourselves in a house or cabin with no power and no way to keep warm except by building a fire. It is at this moment—too late, as it were—that we learn the value of *dry* firewood.

Sure, it seemed easy enough at the time, stacking up that wood outside. Big load of fir, and a guy was selling it alongside the road next to the Piggly Wiggly for 50 bucks. "Dump it in my driveway," you told him. And then you proceeded to spend seven or eight days stacking it up alongside the garage.

A week later, after your third visit to a physical therapist to attempt to regain at least partial function of your lumbar spine, you looked out your window at that 4-by-20-foot blue ribbon of pure emergency preparedness and patted yourself, gingerly, on the back.

It never occurred to you that the cord of wood might be a) greener than the bottom of a produce drawer in a bachelor's refrigerator and b) very likely to stay that way indefinitely, because you failed to cover it in the first place.

That's right. You need to let the wood "cure," or dry. Who knew? Isn't that what bark is for? It doesn't seem fair. But life rarely is.

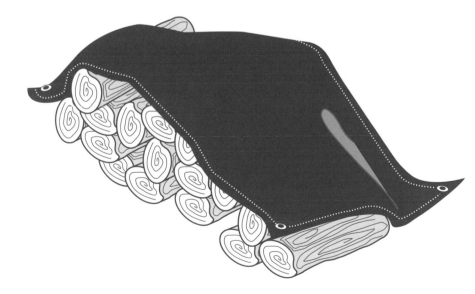

When you go outside to bring in the still-green firewood for your woodstove or fireplace, make sure you get pieces you like. Because you will be staring at them for hours, months, perhaps years, as they smolder, smoke, belch, leak bugs and worms, and do anything a piece of wood can possibly do, short of burning.

Smarter folks will be sitting by a crackling fire in no time, because they found the time a couple years ago to cover the woodpile with a Big Blue Tarp. A *really* big one, folded in such a way that the sides of the pile stay open to the outside air.

That's important. You've gotta let your wood breathe. But keep its head dry with a fine bonnet of bonny blue. And here is the crucial thing: If you want to keep the woodpile's hat on for more than about five minutes, you need to secure the top. In normal climates, you can do this with some old scrap lumber, bricks, or perhaps some big rocks.

In places with exceptional climates, such as Washington State—where the winter wind regularly rips around at speeds a state trooper would take issue with—tarps should be weighed down with scrap lumber, discarded radio towers, a hundred dozen large aluminum ingots spirited away from the nearest shut-down aluminum smelter, and, if available, a yellow 1967 Dodge Polara.

Tarp Application 16

PHOTO/HUNTING BLIND

WHERE:

Anyplace you need to cleverly "conceal" yourself, such as near a duck pond, in a wildlife refuge, or down at the bottom of the driveway of the person you currently are stalking

HERE'S WHERE your common, ordinary Big Blue Tarp approaches the realm of the metaphysical: With the right sort of handiwork, you can turn it into a veritable cloak of invisibility.

No joke.

We're not sure how this works but it must, because hunters have been doing it for eons. Something to do with nature. For instance, if you sat in a lawn chair alongside a pond, wearing camouflage clothing and holding perfectly still, ducks and geese and swans would see you from 150 miles away. You would start hearing their laughter just about the time they reached the Arctic Circle on their southward fall migration, and you would not hear them stop laughing until well after they passed their first Tim Hortons, heading back through Canada in the spring.

But take the same person, in the same pose, in the same place, and cleverly conceal that person behind a large cardboard box with garish blue tarp duct-taped all over it, and no bird known to man would suspect a thing.

"Look," they would say to their buddies after securing a place in the approach pattern to Slimepond International. "There's a large, garish blue object below us, but no people anywhere to be seen! Perhaps we should camp down there."

Whereupon said duck/goose/swan would come in for a landing and waddle close enough to your clever blind for you to reach out and touch it, should you be inclined to do so.

We hate to say it, based on what this says about us as a species, but the same thing works, to a lesser degree, on people. Sure, they might *suspect* that someone is lurking inside the large, garish blue object, but they'll not know for sure. Sooner or later, assuming you refrain from pointing barrels — lens or gun — out of the slit cut in the front of the box for visibility, they'll let their guard down. And this is when you have them.

As usual, there are several ways to construct this cloak of invisibility — all of them wrong if it's a windy day. Here they are, in order of difficulty:

MOST DIFFICULT: Build a frame of local saplings, lashing them together with wire, shoelaces, dental floss, or any other string-like material on hand. Drape tarp(s) over top. It's VERY IMPORTANT to leave one corner of one tarp loose, for ingress and egress. Nobody wants to get stuck inside one of these and have to call 911 on a cell phone for a Jaws of Life emergency duck-blind extrication.

LESS DIFFICULT: Acquire a large refrigerator box from your local appliance store. Cover it with BBTs from top to bottom, then cut a hole in the back. Cut a slit in the front for your rifle and/or long lens. Voilà! Home damp home.

REALLY EASY: Take a 6-foot-by-8-foot BBT with you on your trip. When you reach your destination, unfurl the tarp,

THE BLUE TARP BIBLE

then lie down diagonally in one corner, grab the corner, and roll. Yes, you'll look exactly like a big blue (pork) burrito. But local wildlife, detecting only a large flaming-blue chalupa-like object with a barrel sticking out one end, will be none the wiser!

Oh, did we mention this? Unless you are an official NASA employee trained in the proper use of adult diapers, remember to use the local facilities *before* you seal yourself inside your personal, portable invisibility cloak. You literally don't want to go there.

TARP FAQ

> ### IS "TARP BLUE" AN OFFICIAL CRAYOLA COLOR?
>
> A: **NOT YET.** Write letters, people.

Tarp Application 17

ROOF PATCH AND/OR ENTIRE RESIDENTIAL ROOF

WHERE:

That often-peaked, occasionally flat area at the top of your house that serves as a foundation for your satellite dish, a final resting place for several million cubic yards of leaves and other natural detritus, and at one point kept you dry during rainstorms

WE'VE ALL SAID it at one point or another, driving around (one can hope) someone else's neighborhood: "Holy Bejeebers, look at that two-story brownstone over there. The *entire roof* is a Big Blue Tarp!"

NOTE: The exclamation point at the end of the preceding quotation might be misleading. It is not, in fact, a cry of exultation or admiration, but one of nonfeigned indignation,

i.e., "How in the world can anyone with the common sense God gave a goat think leaving a Big Blue Tarp on a roof is a suitable long-term solution to roof maintenance?"

Possible answers:

1   It may not have been *intended* as a long-term solution. It just seems that way to you and everyone else who, by a terrible twist of fate, doesn't live directly beneath it and thus are left to face the horrific prospect of looking at it every day.

2   Have you *priced* a new roof lately?

3   Well, stuff happens.

We all know people who, on finding themselves with a leaky roof, have made it up on top of the house long enough to string up one Hellaciously Large Blue Tarp, or a series of smaller ones (the overlap and the flow of water can present all sorts of hydrodynamic challenges here), and in the process found the entire ladder/high places/broken limb experience so frightening that they vowed never to go up there again until water starts flowing at flood stage across their LCD bigscreen TV.

The fact is, when your roof starts leaking, you get pretty desperate. And, as has been well established elsewhere in this tome, when water is flowing and your heart rate is rising, few tools are more effective and more expediently available than a trusty BBT.

In fact, if you respond to the small deluge flowing down your kitchen wall by dialing up a certified roofing contractor, he will come over in his $138,000 pickup truck and, while listening to the 24-hour Grateful Dead channel on satellite radio, very likely unfurl a BBT almost identical to the one you could have found lying around in your basement. The difference: His might be a "certified" BBT, with a stamp of approval by some wholly ineffectual government body, such as the Federal Emergency Management Agency.

(How to tell the difference between a FEMA-approved blue tarp and an ordinary, garden-variety blue tarp? The FEMA blue tarp is large, blue, has grommets, and costs $1,250. The everyman's blue tarp is large, blue, has grommets, and costs $3.49.)

The emergency roof patch qualifies as one of the classic BBT deployments: It's a symbolic finger in the dike, a sign that we have trouble here in Rising River City, and we'll get back to it when we darn well please, when our contractor darn well pleases, or when the city threatens to condemn the building, whichever comes last.

Note that the roof patch is one of the straight-on BBT applications: There's no folding, no stringing things up, no building of superstructures, and certainly no heavy lifting. You just lay the sucker out in all its blue glory and nail it to your roof.

Important things to remember:

* The tarp must be *extremely* well nailed down. Usually, a leaky roof is the result of shingles or shakes rotting, then being blown out of place by the sort of winter gale that makes you want to move underground and stay there until spring. BBTs have a propensity to rise and sail off to the next county on a puff of wind no greater than that generated by your spouse slamming the driver's side door of your Daewoo Leganza, so nail 'er down good. We're not saying you should get unduly carried away here: A BBT riddled with nail holes isn't going to do much good against the rain. But if you're at the local rental store looking for a nail gun to tack the sucker down with, get one that's at least a semiautomatic.

* According to Big Blue Tarp etiquette, it's OK to leave the blue tarp on for several days, or months, or years, if you can't get your roof fixed and it's the only thing keeping you dry. But whatever you do, DO NOT become one of those people who cover their entire roof with a BBT, then leave it there so long that the tarp eventually just disintegrates, through the miracle of wind, rain, and sun, into a series of

yards-long locks of polyethylene angel hair, left flapping in the breeze. Doing so will inspire your neighbors and passersby to ponder deep questions, such as: Was the roof ever leaking in the first place, or was the BBT just a preventive measure to *prevent* it from leaking? If the roof was leaking enough to require a BBT patch, how come it isn't leaking again now that the BBT is (for all practical purposes) gone? Did a roof repair crew forget to remove the BBT after finishing the job?

There's another possibility, and it scares us: The roof, either through the power of prayer or the equally miraculous clogging properties of actively growing moss clumps, has healed itself.

Tarp Application 18

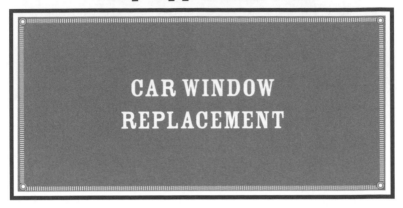

CAR WINDOW REPLACEMENT

WHERE:

Your '68 Buick Electra, or whatever you happen to be driving while you save up for that new Chevy Malibu

THERE ARE THREE KINDS of people in the world:

1   Those who, when the idiot neighbor kid slices a golf ball through their car window, go out and fork over the dough for a new one—or possess insurance with a deductible less than $5,000, making it economically feasible to do so (these are usually management people).

2   Those who, faced with the same dilemma, carefully cut out, shape, and install, using a fine trim of duct

tape, a temporary replacement window made of clear plastic, until a permanent fix can be made.

3   Those who can't afford to buy a new one and can't be troubled enough to manufacture a functional alternative like the one made by that anal-retentive clear-plastic person.

Those of you in the latter category know that nothing says "I don't give a rip and never will" more loudly and clearly than the permanent Big Blue Tarp replacement window.

The beauty of it is you don't even really need to spend the time it took that fastidious clear-plastic guy to cut the plastic into the correct shape. Simply take an old blue tarp of any size greater than the window hole, lay it on top, ask someone to hold it down, and start taping. Put a big strip of duct tape across the top of the square patch. Beauty, eh? Another one on the bottom. Repeat on sides. *C'est magnifique!*

Important scheduling note: This would be a good time to learn how to use your mirrors.

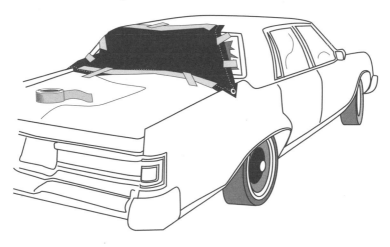

Tarp Application 19

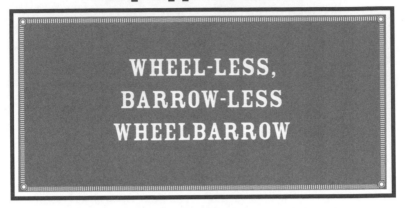

WHEEL-LESS, BARROW-LESS WHEELBARROW

WHERE:

Construction sites, backyards, golf courses, nurseries, the White House, Congress, or anywhere large piles of fertilizer or other refuse needs to be removed and deposited somewhere else

WE USED TO OWN one of those big wheelbarrows with a steel tub and wood handles. Worked like a charm until the first time it got wet, at which point the bottom rusted out and the handles snapped like chopsticks. Then we got one of those wheelbarrows with a plastic tub, a lightweight, rustproof marvel that worked well until we loaded it with something heavier than a geranium leaf, which tore right through the plastic and crashed to the ground.

This kind of guaranteed obsolescence quickly made it clear that the entire wheelbarrow industry was some secret subdivision of Comcast Cable. And, not wanting to further support that corporate entity, we got to thinking: Why not use a Big Blue Tarp?

We'll admit there are serious limits to this application. You cannot, for example, spread out a medium-size blue tarp, place an entire pallet of bricks on it, and pull it across your property. You can, however, use a BBT to move similar amounts of bark, mulch, topsoil, and other common materials.

A couple of beautiful side benefits:

* No unsightly wheelbarrow lying upside down in your backyard like a beached orca.
* Fewer trips between your truck and pile or stack. You can, if you recruit a couple of volunteers to help you pull the tarp, move large heaps of steer manure from one place to another in a single trip.
* You'll be left with a lovely, permanent reminder of your hard work, in the form of a trail of compressed

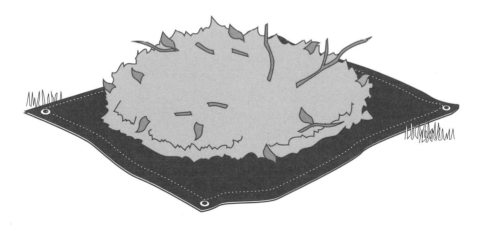

earth, in which nothing is likely to ever grow again—your own homemade skid road. It'll endure longer than most Roman highways and, in extreme cases, will be clearly visible from the International Space Station—assuming the smoke from your smoldering windbreak (see Tarp Application 3) isn't providing sky cover.

TARPS IN THE NEWS

TOPLESS CARWASH HOSES DRIVERS

A handful of young women conducting a car wash riled some customers in the summer of 2007. Their crime? Taking advantage of the Big Blue Tarp's excellent cloaking abilities.

The women, according to Associated Press reports, held up "Topless Car Wash" signs along a highway in Shirley, New York. Drivers who turned in and paid their dough were escorted behind the Big Blue Tarp drapes, where a team of topless—and male—firefighters washed their cars.

"A little bit of bait-and-switch," smirked Donald Prince, the local assistant police chief. "All the guys back there are topless."

Not surprisingly, female customers didn't complain, but more than a few men were miffed that they'd spent their five bucks to watch some burly guys suds it up. Most were mollified when they found out their donation went to a school booster club and other charities.

Tarp Application 20

LANDSCAPING "WATER FEATURE"

WHERE:

Your backyard, front yard, patio, or other outdoor area that, when you think about it, is really just fine exactly the way it is

IT'S ALL THE RAGE these days in landscaping circles. Used to be you were considered a handy landscaper if you could keep a rhododendron alive and the grass down to quiet-riot levels. Now you're nobody unless you have, somewhere on your property, a "water feature," such as a pond, fountain, or other cheeseball squirting apparatus.

Please.

Anyone who's ever spent more than five minutes outside — and yes, we know this rules out 99 percent of the population of Arizona during summer months — knows that "water feature,"

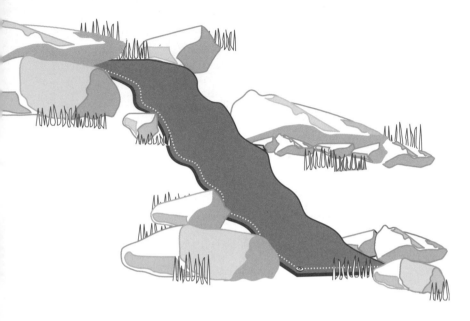

in the language of real life, is spelled t-r-o-u-b-l-e. Bottom line: If it doesn't clog up, it'll freeze. And if it doesn't clog up or freeze, it'll leak, eventually depositing all 117 gallons of its peaceful, gurgling grandeur right into your basement.

Yet even in the face of this incontrovertible logic, someone within your own household—and we're not going to mention names or even sexes here—is going to want to controvert it anyway. Even after acknowledging the folly of it, this person will be unable to resist the urge to keep up with the fountain-spouting Joneses. This person will want a water feature and won't shut up until one is installed and making whatever gargling sound it's going to make.

What to Do? Compromise. Agree to install a water feature on the condition that it is constructed in a manner of your choosing. Then follow these easy steps:

1   Find an outdoor area with a slope sufficient to carry water downhill.

2   Cut a 2-foot-by-10-foot swath of deliciously effervescent blue tarp and lay it on the slope.

3   Gather a dozen or more boulders and a clump or three of moss. Place them in a random fashion along the route of your new "stream."

4   Mix a strong, stiff drink of your choosing, sit back, and admire your handiwork.

If anyone asks, insist that your stream is real and announce that, next spring, you plan to install at its outflow a turbine that will generate enough electricity to power your entire house for free.

Tarp Application 21

WHERE:

Any place on your property you cannot back
your pickup up to

THIS IS PAINFUL TO RECALL, given all the scars, emotional and physical. But as part of our ongoing Post-Himalayan Blackberry Stress Syndrome therapy, we're ready to talk about a long-ago death brush with a brush pile.

It happened right after we moved into our home, around which the contractor, as contractors do, had left us a lovely landscape consisting of a) bulldozer tracks, b) rocks so large they can only be removed with a bulldozer, which, now that your house is built, can never fit onto the property again, and c) a giant, teeming, intimidating mountain of blackberry bushes against the back property line.

Frustrated at our complete inability to address the first two grievances, we set out—decked in protective padding and leather gloves, and armed with a machete and heavy-duty brush loppers—to remedy the third.

Having already struck upon the indisputably ingenious method of moving detritus from one place to another using nothing more than a Big Blue Tarp (see Tarp Application 19), we were thinking unusually far ahead in this case: We would lay out a 16-by-20-foot tarp, anchoring its corners with rocks, and toss the vanquished blackberry vines onto it for later removal.

Long story short: The battle raged for about eight hours. Blood was shed. Roots were pulled. Clothing was torn. Much cursing was heard. But when it ended, that entire mountain of blackberry brambles had been moved from its

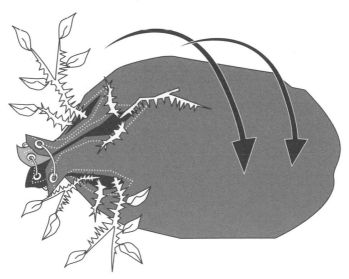

previous location to a new one, a dozen feet away—atop that Big Blue Tarp.

Only one problem: A dramatic underestimation of the weight and bulk of said blackberry mount. No way were we, or any small army for that matter, going to drag this pile to the front of the house and into the pickup for disposal. And even if we could have done that, the fence with the 4-foot-wide gate alongside the house would have proven an insurmountable choke point.

Should you ever find yourself in this situation, consider your three options:

1   Break the pile into numerous small ones, dragging each out on its own tarp.
2   Follow the letter of local burning laws by lighting a 2-by-3-foot "recreational fire." Sit in a lawn chair and roast hotdogs on your simmering brambles for approximately eight weeks, until you run out of brambles—or buns.
3   Cowboy up and roll 'er on out of there.

Choosing the third option, we brainstormed the following plan of attack:

1   Fetch about 30 feet of rope and cut it into four equal lengths. Tie each into a grommet at the tarp corners.
2   Gather up all four ropes, don climbing harness and oxygen mask, and free-climb to the summit of Mount Bramble.
3   Plant flag for Discovery Channel (sponsor). Cinch ropes together as tightly as possible.
4   Descend and admire: a round, blue, ballish object of brambles approximately 12 feet by 10 feet.

In our case, it was *still* too big to drag. So, all the while loudly humming the theme from *Rawhide*, we rolled that bad boy down the hill, up and over the choke-point gate (this took a lot more time than we care to admit, and involved levels of grunting and screaming sufficient to make the neighbors come over and check on us), and down to the front of the house, where, with the aid of sophisticated lever technology and a couple of unsuspecting assistants, it was boosted into the back of the truck to haul to the dump.

It worked. If you choose to undertake such an endeavor yourself, remember our parting advice: Whatever you do, don't forget to close and lock the tailgate.

TARP FAQ

HOW BIG IS AN 8-BY-10 TARP?

A: THOSE OF YOU THINKING "8 FEET BY 10 FEET" are underestimating our propensity for trick questions. The advertised size of a tarp is actually the "finished size." It's like lumber: The real product will be significantly smaller. An 8-by-10 tarp probably was 8 feet by 10 feet at some point in its plasticky life, before it was trimmed and folded over to create side seams. In actuality, the tarp you buy is a couple of inches smaller in both length and width. You've been warned!

WHERE:

A snowy hillside near you — preferably one dotted
by lots of rich kids with expensive Helly Hansen
insulated jackets and even more expensive wood-
and-steel sleds

AROUND OUR HOMETOWN, snowfall during the school
season was a fairly rare thing, and when we did get a good
shellacking of white, it was cause for school closures — and
celebration. During those rare days, someone would be kind
enough to barricade off a couple of hills in town that were too
steep to drive anyway, leaving them for local kids to sled.

A lot of kids had first-rate, newfangled sleds, the kind that,
when you jumped on them from a running start, actually
catapulted down the hill at a rapid pace. And then there were

the rest of us—kids with sleds called Old Rusty, the kind with one runner bowed inward, so that when you got up any speed on it at all, you immediately careened into the ditch, flipped over, and emerged with a large stick going into one side of the back of your jeans and sticking out the other.

Talk about a laughingstock. Not that we're bitter or anything, or that this necessarily led at a later date to prolonged sessions of expensive therapy.

But we digress. One way to avoid the problem of the sticky sled runner, we quickly learned, was to leave the old sled in the garage—or, better yet, feed it, piece by piece, into the campfire at the top of the hill—and turn instead to a trusty BBT.

The tarp had all the slick qualities that kids look for in a toboggan. It was infallible. It was unpredictable. It was highly democratic. It could carry an entire soccer team and still have room to pick up a few more people swept up in the blue wave as it careened downhill. And it was dangerous as hell.

IN OTHER WORDS, IT WAS MAGNIFICENT.

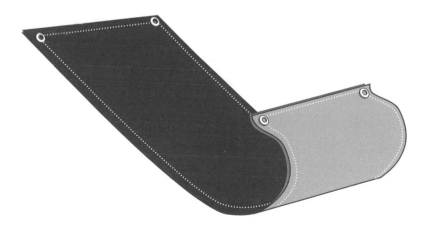

A Big Blue Tarp—we're talking up to 9 feet by 12 feet here, or even bigger for a four-lane street—will slide scary fast down a packed snow slope. And on a hillside groomed to a glare ice surface, which is what our sled hill invariably became after a full day of sledding, it'll shoot downhill like a rocket.

If we had kids, we'd be urging them to make blue tracks down the sled hill on a regular basis, wearing a helmet of some sort and following these specific instructions:

1   Wait for a big crowd of snotty rich kids on expensive new sleds to go down the hill, then start making their way back up.

2   Unfurl your BBT, placing it at the lip of the hill. Find five or six friends, move back 10 yards, and then all run at the thing simultaneously, leaping onto it at the last second and hanging onto it and each other for dear life.

3   Just to ensure they know you're coming, issue a calm, firm audible warning to the people in your path. Something like "AAAAAUUUUUGGGGGHHHHH!"

4   Duck your head before you make contact with their feet, which will become upended as they are turned completely upside down and land on their backsides.

5   Repeat as necessary. And for the love of God, watch out for big rocks.

Tarp Application 23

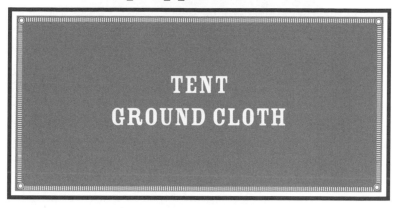

**TENT
GROUND CLOTH**

WHERE:

Beneath your trusty tent, whenever and wherever
it is pitched

THIS IS ONE TO TAKE TO HEART. Of all the uses we've ever conjured up for a BBT, the protective ground floor for a tent is one of the best and one of the simplest. So much so that it's surprising more people don't do it.

We suspect we know why: a) People are stupid, and b) even those who are not stupid fall prey to the marketing hype perpetuated by the outdoor gear industry.

It's an easy mistake to make. Let's say you're at your favorite outdoor store—REI, EMS, Joe's, or what have you—and you're just about to whip out the Visa card for a $350 tent. It's a lot of dough, you think, but heck, it is a six-man tent, which you're buying because, even though it's only you, your significant other, and the dog, everyone knows the "men" they used to measure your "six-man tent" are midgets who would fit four to a 2-pound coffee can.

With this kind of investment, the salesman will suggest, *surely* you want to protect the floor by purchasing the manufacturer's custom-designed, water-repellent, breathable, minty-green colored, coated nylon ground cloth. It's only $49.95, an amount you'd spend three times over if you had to repair a floor rip. Makes sense, right?

Ahem. The ground cloth scam is the tent world's equivalent of selling undercoating on new cars. You *do* need some protection to keep slug slime, sharp rocks, and marshmallow-

laced upchuck from the last family who camped at your site from spoiling your tent floor. But it doesn't have to be coated nylon, and it doesn't have to cost 50 bucks.

Substitute a BBT, and count your savings. **Note:** Splurge and get a brand-new one for this. You want it to be clean and fresh, with that right-out-of-the-bag petroleum-product smell. Buy a tarp that's a couple feet bigger than your tent floor on all sides. Lay it on the ground, and pitch your tent atop it, centering it.

The rest is so simple a 10-term U.S. senator could do it: Simply trace an outline around your tent with a Magic Marker, remove the tent, then cut out the shape. **Tip:** If you cut about six inches *inside* the line, your tent ground cloth will sit just inside the perimeter. Then water dripping down the tent walls will soak into the ground, rather than accumulate between your ground cloth and your tent floor, which gives all new meaning to the word "clammy" when you wake up the next morning.

Your new ground cloth will fold to a small size, fit neatly into the tent stuff sack, and also in a pinch can be used for any of a hundred other emergency blue tarp applications you might need to explore on your next jaunt into the backcountry.

TRUST US: You really can't go wrong here. Well, you could. But only on a snow camping trip, when the ice- and snow-sliding propensities of big blue tarps come into play. See Tarp Application 22, "Blue-Collar Toboggan," and use your best judgment about pitching your tent on a slope. You haven't truly known fear until you've run a giant slalom course in a mummy bag.

Tarp Application 24

TWO-CAR GARAGE

WHERE:

Somewhere outside your house, in a place directly within line of sight of the bay windows of each and every one of your neighbors, but completely out of the line of sight from your house

AT SOME POINT in time, just about everyone finally gets it: That BBT you put over your deceased '66 Camaro nine years ago really doesn't look as good as you had envisioned it would. And now it's time to finally do the right thing:

Raise that baby up.

Nobody likes a tarp lying around forever. But your neighbors are bound to be impressed if you erect one of those newfangled post-and-tarp portable garages with the graceful lines and sheer practicality of a Quonset hut. **Just follow these**

simple steps to seat-of-the-pants architectural greatness:

1   Your new two-car garage will need a frame. You can buy an easy-to-assemble kit, which comes with sections of PVC pipe that can be snapped together. Or, make your own frame by, um, cleaning up after plumbers at that construction site next door and building one from scrap pipe.

2   Once your frame is assembled, recycle the ancient BBT that's been covering your dead car by stretching it over the top and affixing it with bungee cords or rope. Supplement your old blue tarp with six or eight new ones, being mindful that it's useful to leave one end of your garage open for ingress and egress.

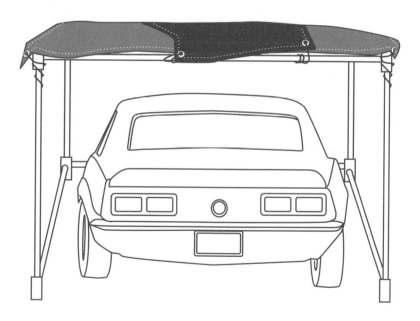

3   Hire gullible neighbor kids to help you push the
     Camaro inside.

4   Smile, rejoice, and consider your options: You could
     acquire another dead '66 Camaro to keep this one
     company. Or park your existing, operational vehicle
     in there. Or, better yet, keep the empty space as
     a sort of funeral-plot-in-reserve for the day your
     existing vehicle becomes nonoperational—very likely
     sometime next week.

TARP FAQ

WHERE DO BLUE TARPS COME FROM?

A: MOSTLY CHINA. Exact figures on the millions
of acres of tarps manufactured every year prove hard
to come by, but everyone acknowledges that the bulk
of the world's BBTs roll off giant Chinese looms, like a
never-ending polyethylene waterfall.

Some tarps are, in fact, manufactured in North
America. And at the risk of trashing Chinese
manufacturing techniques, we can attest that you'll
generally know one of these tarps when you feel one.
North American tarps are thicker, heavier, and bound
to last much longer.

They're also usually more expensive.

But that's another nice thing about the BBT: When it
comes time to shop for one, you generally get what you
pay for.

Tarp Application 25

WALL-TO-WALL TARPETING

WHERE:

Covering every single speck of floor space—and the lower half of wall space—in the home of savvy dog/kid owners

TWO SCHOOLS OF THOUGHT on house-training your new dog/kid:

SCHOOL ONE: Chase after him/her wherever he/she goes, staying ready to scoop up, mop up, or throw up at a moment's notice. Apply several thousand dollars' worth of toxic carpet cleaners to stains. Note that the cleaners will brighten up and clean your carpet stains for better viewing but never, in a million years, take them out.

SCHOOL TWO: Just cut to the chase and put down the Big Blue Tarps before Fido/Zachary ever comes home from the kennel/natural childbirth center.

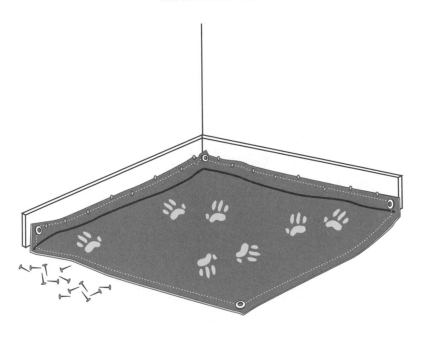

Call us lazy, but we're honor-student grads of School Two. Visitors to our home are asked not to take their shoes off but to leave them on—and cover them with protective plastic booties, like the ones the cable guy puts on when he comes into your house. Except in this case, it's to protect *them* from what's on our floor.

REASON: We had a wonderful dog, Mabel (may she rest in peace), who occasionally had . . . well, accidents in our basement, where she slept. Later, she developed an illness that led to frequent carpet staining—not the grab-a-couple-paper-towels kind, but the call-the-carpeting-contractor kind.

After earning a doctorate in the school of getting carpet stains *almost* out, I decided to cut our losses and just do what any practical polyethylenist would do: install wall-to-wall tarpeting. Worked like a charm, never looked back. **And it can all be done in just a few simple steps:**

1   Clear everything out of the room.
2   Travel to your nearest hardware store and load up on economy blue tarps. Any size will do.
3   Unfurl tarps in the room one by one. Stretch each tarp to the edge of the wall, then pull it up an additional 6–10 inches (depending on height of your dog/kid).
4   Thumbtack the tarp into place along the wall. Place unused heavy objects — some old encyclopedias (kids, ask your parents), those never-lifted barbells, your mother-in-law — on the tarps to secure them.
5   Replace the furniture, being mindful as you carry one end of that twelve-ton sleeper sofa that a blue tarp underfoot can be slicker than a banana slug smooshed between two sheets of waxed paper (again, don't ask).
6   Stand by and watch, with complete and utter smug satisfaction (the kind where you fold your arms across your chest) as your dog/kid tries to stain the carpet through your brilliantly conceived wall-to-wall tarpet defense shield. See the look of defeat in his/her eyes and laugh maniacally.

SADLY, WE HAVE ACTUALLY DONE THIS. AND IT WORKS.
Note: The tarps will seem unduly crinkly underfoot until you get used to them, and you will need to pull them up and

take them outside for hosing/pressure washing every few weeks. But that's all the maintenance required.

And just think: eighteen years from now, when the dog/kid is gone for good, you'll have brand-spanking-new, pristine carpeting—in a two-decades-old style.

Where did you leave that phone number for the carpet contractor again?

TARP FAQ

WHAT CAME FIRST, THE BLUE TARP OR "TARP BLUE"?

Welcome to one of the greatest existential quandaries of our time. It gets right to the heart of the question that defines our universe, namely: Who made the blue tarp that (pick one) beautiful/garish/alluring/alarming shade of electric blue?

A: NOBODY REALLY KNOWS. Tarps come in a rainbow of colors: silver, white, red, green, gray, camouflage, yellow, brown, black—even U-Haul orange. But the vast majority of tarps sold worldwide are "tarp blue."

Why? In our extensive research, we've seen all sorts of speculation. Among the popular answers:

* Blue tarps, because they often serve maritime purposes, were originally made to emulate the deep blue color commonly used for boating gear, ▶▶▶

particularly sail bags, sail covers, and awnings. (A very plausible explanation.)

* The color is a completely random, computer-created choice that became immortalized when some guy in some lab in China pushed some buttons several decades ago. (Very possibly true — in fact, the most likely explanation.)

* It's a basic "construction" color favored by contractors. Sort of a subliminal message that says "work in progress." (Doubtful.)

* Add your own theory here.

Here's what we *do* know: Far greater minds than ours, including reporters from the *Washington Post* and an esteemed colleague, William Dietrich, Pulitzer-prize–winning reporter for *The Seattle Times*, have attempted, and failed, to solve the mystery of tarp blueness.

In a 2006 treatise on the Big Blue Tarp in the newspaper's *Pacific Northwest Magazine,* Dietrich put the question to no less an authority than C. R. Skidmore, president of tarp manufacturer DIZE Co. Skidmore's response: "It just seems that people like blue."

Likewise, Dietrich got no help from other luminaries from the world of plastics, including representatives of DuPont and Dow, a national plastics museum, or plastics-industry lobbying groups.

Other tarp makers thought a federal agency, such as FEMA, mandated the color. But the agency never responded to Dietrich's questions, leading him to surmise: "They're still, we suspect, grumpy about the whole hurricane thing."

Tarp Application 26

DUVET COVER

WHERE:

Your master suite, wherever it might be and whoever might master it

LET'S SAY YOU'RE AN AVERAGE American male who works hard, pays his taxes, and yeah, so what, likes to dine on the occasional Chef Boyardee product in bed while enjoying reruns of *Saved by the Bell*.

Your partner is an average American female who, on a daily basis, wonders how in the hell she ever wound up with you, and whether there's any hope you can be retrained before she eventually bounces you out on your ear where you belong.

There's a middle ground, people—a happy, in-between bit of real estate in Compromise City.

It's the Big Blue Tarp Duvet Cover (patent pending).

Now, before you blanch with disgust, ladies, consider the trade-offs here. We know that putting a Big Blue Tarp over your 800-fill Hungarian goose down comforter, with its true

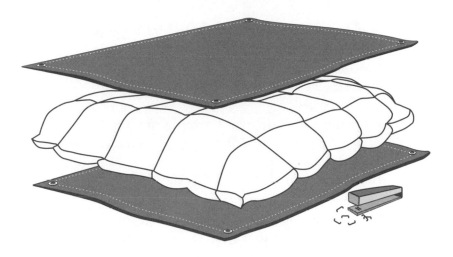

channel box construction and 1,250-thread count woven Egyptian cotton cover, might seem like framing a Monet with old sections of slot-car racetrack.

But think about the upside: A duvet cover fashioned from tarps—no matter the color, and never mind those corner grommets, which can be startlingly cold when they brush up against your bare, exposed torso at night—is still a lot better looking than what passed for bedding on your man's bed before you came along.

Plus, it'll be 100-percent resistant to Beefaroni, chili con queso sauce, bean dip, and Miller Genuine Draft.

It's up to you. Cling to the illusion that you can change him—or employ suitable defenses.

Just take a deep breath, concede the inevitable, and follow these simple instructions:

1 Purchase two new, still plasticky-smelling Big Blue Tarps. Four-by-six-footers should suffice for twin or

double beds. Use six-by-eight-footers for a queen- or king-size bed.*

2   Lay one tarp out on the floor. Spread your beautiful goose-down comforter across it (chili stains down). Weep.

3   Place the other tarp over the top. Continue weeping.

4   Staple. Staple. Staple. Staple. Staple. Staple. Staple. Staple. Staple. Staple.

5   Finish weeping.

Sooner than you think, you will get used to your new duvet cover and won't be able to wait to slide beneath that all that cold, crinkly, plasticky, 100-percent-guaranteed stain-proof splendor.

If you have difficulty getting over the fashion hurdle, remember that you can dress up your tarp duvet with an accompanying dust ruffle, in keeping with the same general theme. A canvas drop cloth comes to mind.

---

* If you have a "Select Comfort" or "Sleep Number" bed with an inflatable mattress, throw your entire bed in the dumpster and just sleep on the tarps instead. It'll be just as comfortable, and you'll never have to fiddle with silly headboard controls.

Tarp Application 27

KAYAK

WHERE:

Any local waterway, though preferably one within
life ring–tossing distance of a well-equipped Coast
Guard cutter or other suitable rescue craft

THIS ONE BEGINS WITH A DISCLAIMER: We would
not ever, in a million years, actually get into one of these
kayaks—not even if we were stuck on an island somewhere,
an entire boatload of Jehovah's Witness missionaries was
about to land, and it was the only way off.

Having said that: It has been reported to us that large
numbers of American citizens, living up to the current
National Motto ("We've Really Got Nothing Else to Do"),
have fashioned usable, somewhat navigable kayaks using
nothing more than Big Blue Tarps, bailing wire, and sticks.

You could laugh, or you could get on the Internet and dial
up *http://www.shelter-systems.com/kayak.html,* where you will
find complete instructions. So there.

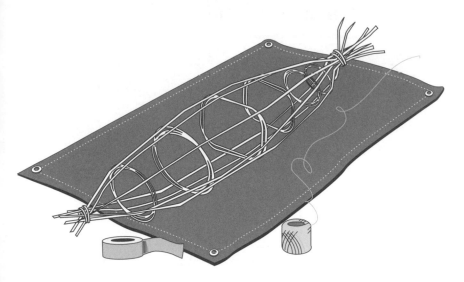

Essentially, you take many long strips of green willow or other suitable branches, tie them in hoops that serve as the ribs, then run longer strips of the same up both sides. Secure these strips at the ends with wire, string, or rawhide.

When the frame is finished, it resembles a packing crate for an unusually large cucumber — or perhaps the frame for a caveman-constructed dirigible.

NEXT STEP: Wrap blue tarp all around it, binding the open seams at the top with Grip Clips, duct tape, or some other fastening device, and either leaving or cutting a hole large enough for you to squeeze into. The finished hand-fashioned watercraft has all the cuddly attributes of an overweight cat at the pet shelter: It only weighs about 20 pounds, and it can be yours for practically nothing.

Add your own paddle, and you're ready for the high seas or whitewater.

Important safety disclaimer: Unless you have considerable experience piloting a pile of sticks and wad of blue tarp through dangerous whitewater, consider sticking to the off-whitewater for the time being.

FINAL NOTE: On the website describing the BBT kayak, we noticed that, near the end of the instructions, beneath a picture of the designer with his craft—which resembles a coffin for a ruler of the ancient Egyptian Tarp Dynasty—he comments that the kayak is "good-looking." This proves that there truly is no accounting for taste.

TARPS IN THE NEWS

ARCHITECTS WHO KNOW THEIR ROOTS...ALL TOO WELL

When the American Institute of Architects' Alaska chapter held its state convention at the Alyeska Princess Hotel in 2005, it chose as one convention theme "Beyond Blue Tarp." There was even a photo contest held around the topic of "the notorious use of blue tarps in Alaska."

Tarp Application 28

TRUCK-BED LINER LINER

WHERE:

The nether regions of your Dodge, Ford, Chevy, Nissan, or Toyota pickup

HERE'S WHAT HAPPENS to someone who buys a new pickup truck and has a bullet-proof, rock-proof, dirt-proof, rain-proof, chemical-proof, fire-proof, spray-on bed-lining material applied to the bed.

The truck bed, once just a space for hauling stuff, suddenly looks nice. Very nice. Too-nice-to-wreck-by-hauling-a-dirty-rototiller nice.

It's ironic, yes. But applying a lifetime protective coating that allows you to haul anything from spent nuclear fuel rods to molten lava in your pickup bed may actually result in your complete and utter inability to haul anything, ever.

Relax: You're just one Big Blue Tarp away from lining your liner and losing your inhibitions. You'll only need four large cement blocks and four bungee cords.

Then follow these steps:

1. Spread the Big Blue Tarp over the top of your $1,200, never-touched spray-on lining in the truck bed.
2. Secure the BBT at all four corners with cement blocks.
3. Run the bungee cords through the grommets in the top corners and secure them to the bedrail tie-downs.

Haul away. The BBT bed liner can be changed easily, and it has a special added feature for hauling garbage: When you arrive at the dump and you're in a hurry, just unhook your bungee ties, back up really fast, and slam on the breaks. The whole thing—garbage, liner, blocks, the works—is guaranteed to come out in one large pile, from which you can quickly speed away as if you have no idea how it got there.

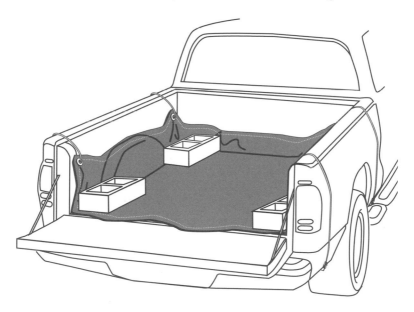

Legal disclaimer: The author of this book would NEVER recommend doing this in a turnout along a little-traveled country road, or anywhere elsewhere you don't have to pay through the nose to plug your nose and dump your garbage.

NOTE: This BBT application is not without drawbacks. When you're driving your truck on the freeway, your liner liner will blow and bellow and rattle and sound like a boom box being fed through a tree-limb shredder while playing MC Hammer. Either get used to this, or get in the habit of driving around with several yards of topsoil in the back. It'll help with your winter traction anyway.

Also, when you slam on your brakes really, really hard, the cement blocks in the back of the bed will come flying forward with the force of the Space Shuttle going through reentry. If either of these two blocks penetrates the rear wall of your truck cab, then Dude, you were really driving too fast to begin with.

TARP TRIVIA

BIG BLUE TARP ETIQUETTE

Let's face it: Staring at a Big Blue Tarp—especially if it's one across the street, at your neighbor's house—is like looking at the sun. It's OK when you see it in your peripheral vision, but stare directly at it for too long and it'll scorch your eyeballs.

Given this, it's important, not to mention neighborly, to follow some basic rules of tarp etiquette, which we admittedly just now made up for this occasion, but which no ▶▶▶

doubt soon will be written into city ordinances, homeowner's association covenants, and United Nations agreements:

* Maximum time you can leave a BBT covering your car/trailer/RV/boat in a prominent, street-visible location: six months. That's the point at which your neighbors, seeing leaves falling from trees, will recognize that they've lived with your BBT for two entire seasons, and their patience will run out. (**Note:** Truly massive blue tarps—those covering RVs or boats of 40 feet or more—should be removed in an even more timely fashion. Good rule of thumb: Remove it in three hours or less after the first time you overhear a neighbor refer to your family as "the tarp people.")
* Maximum BBT coverage allowance for woodpiles: two years, roughly. The woodpile tarp is less obtrusive. But if you haven't burned through your wood in two years, you don't really need a woodpile, do you?
* Maximum window for a "temporary" BBT roof repair: three months. Double-time exemption: Hurricane zones, where even those people wealthy and motivated enough to put on a new roof will never be able to find a qualified roofing contractor.

You can argue with these rules if you want. Even attempt to flout them. Just don't come running to us when somebody "accidentally" lights your highly flammable plastic sheeting on fire.

Tarp Application 29

MAN PURSE

WHERE:

Over your shoulder, Pardner

IT'S AN AGE-OLD DILEMMA. As an active American guy who travels a lot, you've got a lot of stuff to keep track of: car keys; plane tickets; credit cards; bubble gum; passport; grooming kit; dry-cleaning tickets; Just For Men applicator brush; phone numbers that, for the life of you, you can't attach to any person you've ever met; spare change; contraceptive devices; Get-Out-of-Jail-Free card (you never know); jerky strips; dental floss; Starbucks gift card with 39 cents remaining credit; Junior Ranger Certification card; iPod; Leatherman tool; and 1977 and 2007 ticket stubs from Styx concerts.

You could try—in fact, you have tried—to fit this all into your wallet, which is possible, but creates such a thick pile that you're left cocked 45 degrees to one side whenever you're seated. Or you could wear a small pack, which works fine, assuming you want to spend your life with a small river of sweat flowing down the center of your back.

Some designers have gone so far as to design a male "organizer bag" that holds all your stuff within reach—at the bottom of a strap hanging from your shoulder. But let's be honest: Not even those most secure in their masculinity are going to be caught dead buying rebar at Home Depot and paying for it with a Visa card fished from a man purse.

No way.

But you can maintain your swarthy, sweat-stained dignity by fashioning a man purse out of that material that simply reeks of testosterone: BBT fabric.

Follow these simple steps to male greatness:

1   Purchase, purloin, or otherwise acquire a small blue tarp, a glue gun, a stapler, and a three-foot length of clothesline.

2   Cut out a 12-by-24-inch rectangle of tarp.

3   Fold it in half to make a one-foot square.

4   Temporarily unfold the tarp material. Place glue along the two sides, leaving the top open and being sure to burn yourself with the hot glue gun as you do so. Refold.

5   Watch *SportsCenter* several times until the glue dries.

6   Placing the open end up, staple the ends of the clothesline to the top corners of the pouch to make a stylish shoulder strap.

7   Take your new man purse outside and drop it in cow manure. Step on it. Spray it with fish guts. Stomp on it. Back over it with your truck. Light it on fire. In short: Do whatever's necessary to remove any trace of newness or tidiness.

8   Put your stuff inside, sling the bag over your shoulder, and get on with your life — better equipped and certainly more balanced from side to side.

Aside from never being separated from life's little essentials, there's another beautiful benefit: Nobody will ever mess with a guy wearing a blue-tarp man purse. He simply looks too crazy to approach. You never know what he might be packing in there.

TARPS IN THE NEWS

BURN, BLUE BABY, BURN

We've already mentioned Operation Blue Roof, the U.S. government's attempt to patch up homes and businesses slammed by hurricanes in the Gulf states.

One unintended consequence of that sea of blue didn't come to light until later, when New Year's Eve rolled around. Local fire marshals worried that that sea could turn red in an instant if blue tarps were ignited by wayward fireworks.

As reporter Sonja Isger pointed out in the *Palm Beach Post*:

On New Year's Eve, fire chiefs regularly curse Mother Nature's version of kindling—all those dried pine needles and leaves atop roofs. This year, those chiefs have an added concern: thousands of blue tarps.

Turns out they burn.

And while they may take longer to catch fire than a pile of straw, once they do, they drip flames, spew toxic fumes and can be tough to extinguish.

Local firefighters conducted a demonstration, using a scale model, and the results weren't pretty.

As the story notes: *While the tarps have proven their worth in keeping rain out, fire dripping from a tarp into a hole in the roof would be a firefighter's nightmare. And when it came time to douse the demonstration fire, the stream of water let loose a burst of flames instead.*

MORAL: Roman candles and big blue tarps definitely don't mix.

Tarp Application 30

TABLECLOTH

WHERE:

A picnic table, the hood of your car, or, better yet, in the middle of an expensive wedding or baptismal ceremony at a local city park

RED CHECKS are so Dorothy-in-Kansas.

Which is why, the next time you feel the uncontrollable urge to prepare a meal, pack it up, haul it away from home comforts such as flatware, chairs, tables, and your flat-screen, and actually eat it *outside*, where bugs and things that eat bugs live, you should leave that old fabric tablecloth where it belongs. In the closet.

You don't even need to pack a tarp, because, if you're anywhere close to handy, you already have one in the trunk, underneath the spare tire.

Once you get to your destination, haul out the BBT, spread it out, light the candles, and yell "Bon appétit!"

Size recommendations:

* Dinner for two: a 4-by-6-footer (grommets folded underneath)
* Casual dinner for four: one at least 8 feet by 10 feet, grommets up (doubling as olive holders)
* Big family reunion spread: the king-size 30-by-40-footer, folded once lengthwise (no plates necessary—just turn it over for dessert).

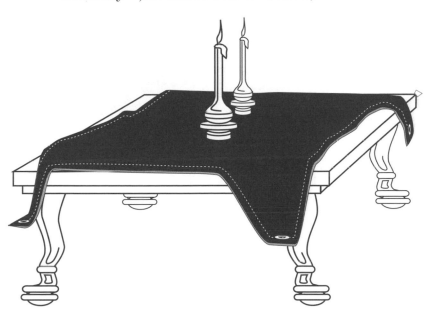

Tarp Application 31

WATER COOLER

WHERE:

Outside or, if you work for a not-for-profit, in your office

A WHILE BACK, we heard someone commenting that, with so many people now working at home, on the road, or on the beach (management people, you know who you are), there's really a lot less office "water cooler" conversation than there used to be. Now a second death blow has been dealt to water coolers everywhere: competition from those ubiquitous and utterly nonsensical personal water bottles.

What most office jaw-flappers probably fail to realize is that the once-proud tradition of shooting the breeze around a water cooler can be replicated outdoors—or indoors, if you're truly handy—using common materials. To wit:

* One medium-size blue tarp
* 6 inches of bailing wire
* 10 to 20 feet of rope

* One large tree, house frame, or other tall object —
  or a beefy swag hook for indoor applications
* One .22-caliber rifle or similar firearm
* 20 or 30 gallons of water

You're probably way ahead of us here, but follow these steps anyway:

1   Gather the tarp's four corners together and affix
    them with bailing wire. Tie one end of the rope to the
    bailing wire. Fill the tarp with water. Throw the other
    end of the rope over the tall object, or loop it over the
    ceiling hook.
2   Hoist!
3   Move back 20 feet.
4   Shoot the blue-tarp water sack with the .22 rifle.

5   Stand beneath the flowing stream, fill up a collapsible paper cup, and ask the guy next to you: "Did you see that dreamy episode of *Grey's Anatomy* last night?"

6   Repeat as necessary until the water runs out or the guy next to you files a complaint with the human resources department, whichever comes first.

TARPS IN THE NEWS

HIGH-TECH NASA TURNS TO LOW-TECH PROTECTION

In September 2005, with Hurricane Rita bearing down on the Gulf states, NASA technicians at some of the nation's most prized bastions of high technology were scrambling to protect valuable components. And on that score, they ranked right there with the rest of us.

As reported by Space.com writer Tariq Malik:

Meanwhile, 40 emergency personnel hunkered down at NASA's New Orleans-based Michoud Assembly Facility, where space shuttle external tanks are built, while a skeleton crew watched over Stennis Space Center in Mississippi.

NASA officials said Michoud crews were using nets and blue tarps to shield shuttle fuel tanks from damage during the impending storm. Stennis officials expected heavy rain and wind from Hurricane Rita.

Tarp Application 32

WEEDKILLER

WHERE:

Anywhere weeds grow, which, where we live, is
literally everywhere outside, and a few places inside

OF THE TWO HIGHLY EFFECTIVE WAYS we know to
kill a large volume of weeds without accidentally spraying
other, valued plant life nearby, one of them has a rather
substantial problem:

Last time we checked, it was illegal to call in a napalm air
strike on a batch of cheatgrass.

That leaves you with the lone sensible alternative: Death
by tarp.

Over the many tens of thousands of years of human
existence—or over the many weeks of same, if you're one of
those geniuses who believes the world is only 6,000 years old—
it has become well established that, if you cover something with
a tarp for long enough, that something eventually will die.

Hence an easy, cost-effective solution for killing grass, weeds, or your neighbor's predatory morning glory vines: Tarp it all over.

One good 20-by-30 tarp can take out a front lawn in about two months. Lay 'er flat, lash 'er down, and set your watch.

While you're waiting, pretend you suddenly have become the proud owner of lakefront property. Celebrate the occasion by erecting an unsightly boathouse and hosting a beach party, complete with steel-drum band and limbo dancing.

Nobody has ever had that much fun spraying RoundUp.

Tarp Application 33

JED CLAMPETT ROOFTOP CARRYALL

WHERE:

On top of your car, usually on a camping trip, during an "adventure in moving," or on the way home from the airport

COMMON PROBLEM: Trunk too small for luggage/ camping gear/college dorm belongings. Easy solution: Sleek, aerodynamic Big Blue Tarp rooftop carrier.

Follow these why-didn't-I-think-of-that steps:
1 Get a tarp large enough to wrap once—preferably twice— around the items to be hauled.
2 Unfurl the tarp on the roof of your car.
3 Walk 12 blocks north and retrieve the tarp from where it has been blown by a tiny puff of wind.

4   Put it back on the roof of the car.

5   Stack the items on top of the tarp. General rule of thumb: Don't stack higher than twice the original height of your car.

6   Wrap the loose ends of the tarp up and over the items and down the sides of the roof, being careful not to obscure windows.

7   Cover the entire gigantic Blue Rooftop Blob with several lengths of rope or, better yet, one of those slick spiderweb bungee covers from an auto parts store.

8   Secure the ends of the rope/webbing inside the cab of the car, through the open windows.

9   Close the windows. Assign your roommate/significant other/someone who doesn't know any better to sit in the backseat and hold on tight to any loose ends.

10 Drive fast. True, this increases the potential for Blue Rooftop Blob drift or, in worst-case scenarios, even decoupling. But it decreases the probability that you'll be spotted by an overeager state trooper. If an officer of the law does stop you to inquire about the load, remain calm, look him/her in the eye, and insist you have no idea whatsoever how the stuff got on top of

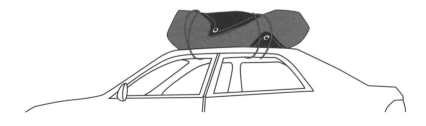

your car, but you will gladly take it off as soon as you get to where you're going.

NOTE: The BBT rooftop carryall is a temporary measure and should never be used to move large items halfway across the United States. You could smash everything to bits, and, as everyone knows, we already have the U.S. Postal Service for that.

TARPS IN THE NEWS

WARNING: YOUR BIG BLUE TARP IS NOT A TOY!

A Plymouth, Massachusetts, man found out the hard way that a BBT can, under the right conditions, be guilty of attempted homicide.

According to an account in the Quincy, Massachusetts, *Patriot Ledger*, the man was out raking leaves at a rental cottage, piling them onto a tarp, then throwing them off a cliff into Cape Cod Bay, when someone noticed he had disappeared.

Neighbors soon spotted the man—two-thirds of the way down the side of the cliff. He'd been trying to toss the leaves on the tarp over the edge and had fallen into the abyss.

After a rescue by Coast Guard helicopter, the tarp flinger escaped with only minor head and arm injuries. The condition of the tarp was not available at press time.

Tarp Application 34

FIVE-MINUTE RAIN FLY

WHERE:

In your campsite or at your local picnic area on
an unexpectedly rainy day

YOU ALL KNOW THE DRILL. You're sitting around a
campfire on a partly cloudy day that forecasters had been
promised would be sunny—typically a holiday.

Someone to your left says the dirty words. "Was that
rain?"

Pandemonium ensues, as you and four friends/relatives
run for the trunk of the car for the essentials: A Big Blue Tarp
and an accompanying Big Tangled Wad of Clothesline.

Having pitched camp strategically in a spot with three or
more trees adjacent to the picnic table and fire pit, you're
already mentally prepared for this. One section of clothesline
goes up over that branch, another around that tree trunk,
one on top of that light post, the last one on top of the two
tent poles jury-rigged together with twist ties off the top of

the hamburger bun package. Lash down the clothesline and throw the tarp over the top, securing it with clothespins, duct tape, or whatever you can find.

Less than 30 minutes later, you will be...soaked, but sitting in a dry space, under your tarp, next to the campfire, thawing out and reminding your friends/relations just how lucky they are to be with someone so highly skilled at the art of self-preservation.

And then it will start to rain harder, and it will begin: Water will begin to migrate from your tarp's strategically situated high points and, thanks to the twin miracles of gravity and inevitability, begin to pool up in low spots you could not have envisioned.

This will continue for 20 or 30 minutes, at which point the tarp will give up, shift suddenly and, as if on purpose, drop that

entire load of water, much like an air tanker on a wildfire, right on top of your Aunt Rose, who will scream and fling her flaming bratwurst off the end of her stick, sending a heat-seeking sausage missile into the adjacent campsite, hitting a personal-injury attorney in the face and possibly putting his eye out.

Nobody ever said camping was for the faint of heart.

TARP FAQ

JUST HOW MUCH BLUE TARP IS OUT THERE?

A: THAT'S UNCLEAR. Because BBT fabric is produced in such quantities in so many spots around the globe, it's tough to get a handle on current production levels. Some U.S. manufacturers report making more than 50 million yards of tarp a year, and production from Chinese factories likely dwarfs that number.

Here's what we figure: There's enough blue tarp out there right now that, if you duct-taped it all together, you could cover a significant portion of New Jersey — which, when you think about it, might not be such a bad idea.

Tarp Application 35

TRUCK LOAD COVER

WHERE:

Over the top of old tires, rotting wood, the crumpled, rotting remains of your Halloween 2005 pumpkin, or whatever else you're finally getting around to hauling to the dump after a brief delay of 18 months

IT USED TO BE that "covering your load" in a pickup truck or a flatbed on the way to a refuse facility was just common courtesy. Now, it's far more serious.

As in: If your Halloween 2005 jack-o'-lantern should fly out of your moving vehicle and bean an innocent bystander, they can throw you in jail.

So pay attention.

In most states, you *must* cover an open load of whatever you're hauling or risk a ticket. And if you're going to do it,

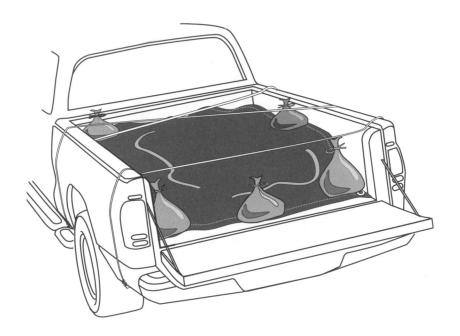

might as well do it right: With a Big Blue Tarp that, if you tie it on like most people do, will do absolutely nothing to cover your detritus but will billow out behind your car like a flailing spinnaker on a sailing sloop, signaling to police cars and all passersby that, well, you *tried* to cover it up.

And that's really what it's all about, right?

Seriously: We can't honestly recommend a Big Blue Tarp as a truck load cover because, for whatever reason, tarps and the backs of pickup trucks are clearly two diametrically opposing forces of nature. The minute the tarp gets put on, the load and the truck begin to conspire together about how to get the damn thing off. And they almost always succeed.

You can have the tarp secured with several dozen ropes, a virtual spider's web of bungee cord, twenty or thirty sandbags, and occasional spot welds, and it still won't matter. Five minutes down the road, the corners will work loose. A minute after that, the back half will be flapping happily in the breeze. And two minutes after that, 99 percent of the tarp will be blazing away behind you, like some demonic blue flame.

Take heart in knowing it isn't you or anything you've done. It's just one of the cold, hard facts of Blue Tarp Life.

Look at the bright side: Yes, eventually, that dancing, mocking tarp will work its way loose, in the process loosening the ropes holding everything else on. But, thanks to your stupendous foresight in load management, when you go searching through two counties for the goods that fell out of your truck, you won't just be looking for a banged-up wheelbarrow. You'll be looking for a banged-up wheelbarrow with a Big Blue Tarp still clinging, with great determination, to one end.

Take it from an experienced hunter of wheelbarrow remains: It's the difference between night and day.

Tarp Application 36

SAIL

WHERE:

In place of your mainsail, topsail, spinnaker, you name it, on your beloved sailboat

IN THE SAILBOAT WORLD, there's cheap, and then there's hoisting-up-the-blue-tarp-mainsail cheap.

Not that there's anything wrong with that. In fact, in a social circle as awash in cash as the sailing world, it's darnright refreshing to have someone come along and slip the occasional turd in the punchbowl, as it were.

Besides, we know from personal experience that many sailors are not trust funders—at least not after sinking the considerable bulk of their savings into a sailboat—and in fact boast something of a renegade spirit.

This explains why those intrepid souls who build their own sailing dinghies from plywood and silicone rubber, with a homemade mast flying sails cut from blue tarps (or Tyvek home wrap) tug at the heartstrings of even the most well-heeled sailor. And why a guy who sailed the entire East Coast of the United States using only blue tarp sails became an instant dock-talk legend.

The infamous Captain Freddie, the story goes, sailed a fiberglass cruiser with all-blue-tarp sails from Massachusetts to Florida. Rumor has it that he is now holed up in the Northeast writing a book about his polytarp-sail wanderings.

Cheap tarp sails have become so popular, in fact, that a garage-based business in Indiana, PolySail International, now sells tarp sails (alas, they're sail white, not tarp blue) to thrifty sailors worldwide. We won't pretend to match their expertise, nor attempt to invade their commercial turf. But you can check out the company yourself online at *http://members.aol.com/polysail/HTML/index.htm.*

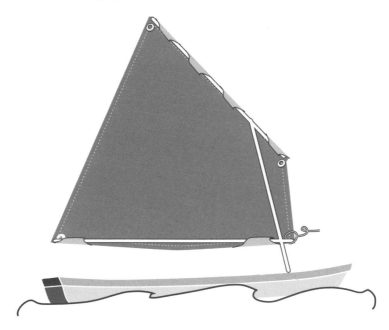

Note that you don't need a large sloop in your backyard to have fun with tarp sails. The company sells a 7-by-10-foot sail kit you can affix to a common canoe.

But you don't even really need a watercraft of any kind to use your trusty tarp to harness the wind.

When you're out on skis or skates on a frozen lake in the winter, with a big tailwind boosting you right along, how many times have you wondered what it would be like to hoist a blue tarp mainsail between your ski poles and *really* get moving?

To borrow a line from Warren Miller: If you don't try it this winter, you'll only be a year older when you do.

TARP FAQ

HOW LONG HAVE BBTS BEEN AROUND?

A: IN THEIR CURRENT FORM, SINCE THE 1970S. Before the plastics revolution, most tarps were made from cotton or hemp canvas. Some of these are still around, and you'll know one when you see it — or attempt to lift it. Cotton canvas is at least five times as heavy as polyethylene, many more times that when it's wet. Unlike plastic, it mildews easily. And as anyone who's spent many nights in an old cotton-canvas tent (a few are still out there) will tell you, it's not nearly as waterproof. Most stubborn cotton-tent campers today, in fact, equip their abodes with a waterproof tarp — a big blue one comes to mind — as a seat-of-the-pants rain fly.

Tarp Application 37

DRAG CHUTE

WHERE:

At the rear end of any object moving entirely too fast for comfort, such as a speeding car, bicycle, snowmobile, or skateboard—or perhaps your career in the investment banking industry if you sunk all your money into Chinese lead paint futures

THIS MIGHT BE AN ANTIDOTE for many of the other Big Blue Tarp applications herein that involve building up significant amounts of speed. It's also one of the trickier items to make, thus it is recommended only for the most highly skilled in the arts of tarpage.

To wit:

1   Base the size of your drag chute on the relative size of the item you wish to "drag." For instance, a drag chute for a top-fuel funny car should utilize the largest tarp immediately available, whereas one

for, say, a Barbie Ferarri might be as small as the circumference of your head.

2   Cut the tarp into an octagon shape. Don't ask us how to do this. We never did very well in geometry.

3   Affix at each of the eight corners—octagon equals eight, yes?—a long strand of zip cord or other strong, lightweight rope.

4   Connect the ends of the rope to the rear end of the item to be dragged.

5   Deploy at the moment of Maximum White Knuckleage.

6   Hope for the best.

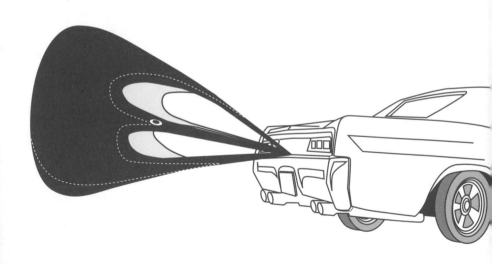

Tarp Application 38

INDUSTRIAL-STRENGTH ZIPLESS FREEZER BAGGIE

WHERE:

In your deep freeze or walk-in freezer

SO LET'S SAY you've got a hindquarter of a large moose lying there on the kitchen table.

Having already consumed a matching moose hindquarter over the last couple of days—forty-eight hours filled with moose stew, moose sausage, moose pancakes, moose salad, moose burgers, moose pizza, moose omelets, and, for dessert, moose mousse—the thought of downing another one ranks right up there with undergoing an IRS audit.

SOLUTION: Freeze it.

Now, we won't even begin to speculate how much chopping, grinding, and pulverizing might be necessary to get all that moose into seven or eight thousand zipper bags of the size you'll find at your local Piggly Wiggly. Wiser souls cut to the chase and vacuum pack the Big Blue Tarp way.

Follow these simple steps:

1   Lay one large blue tarp in the middle of the kitchen floor.
2   Place the moose hindquarter—or other gigantic meat object—atop one end of the tarp.
3   Pull the other half of the tarp over the intimidating, rank meat pile, as if you're tucking it into bed. (Goodnight kiss: optional.)
4   Apply silicone sealant or other airtight/watertight goop—possibly the contents of several dozen Jell-o Snack Pudding pouches—to the inside edges of the tarp, leaving a 2-inch gap in one corner.
5   After the goop dries, insert the nozzle of your shop vac in the corner opening. Turn on the vacuum; observe the vacuum action as the intimidating, rank meat pile is shrink-wrapped in luscious blue tarp.

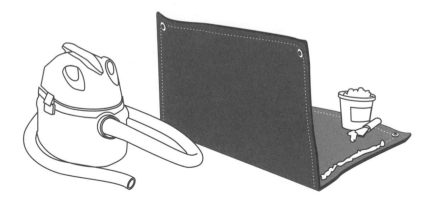

6   Remove the nozzle, fold over the corner, and quickly seal it with the remaining goop.
7   Open the freezer door and use a forklift or several burly family members to boost the big blue meat glob into the freezer.
8   To thaw: Repeat in reverse order.

NOTE: There's an added advantage to tarp freezing over traditional vacuum packing. Your meat comes out with something it would never ordinarily have: a geometrically perfect texture of tiny adjoining squares—and a freezer-burned-grommet brand right in the center.

Tarp Application 39

UNABOMBER TARPAPER-SHACK MOOD SKYLIGHT

WHERE:

Aforementioned Tarpaper Shack
(aka Your Rustic Hideaway in the Woods)

EVERYONE CAN RELATE to the feeling: After living in an underground hole or a windowless tarpaper shack in the backcountry for several years, you start to get moody. In fact, prolonged spans without any exposure to the sun's rays might make you downright cranky. Next thing you know, you're sending letter bombs to the nation's leading technical wizards.

Not that this has actually happened or anything. But you can see it, right?

Our aim, as always, is prevention. The next time you realize you can't remember the last time you saw natural light inside the place you reside, follow these simple steps:

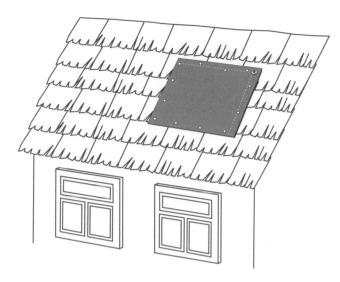

1   Using a jigsaw or handsaw, cut a 4-foot-square hole in your roof.

2   From the outside—yes, we know getting here is a big step for some of you—cover the hole with a 6-by-6-foot blue tarp.

3   Staple or nail the edges.

4   Slink back inside and look up. Rather than solid darkness, a soft, calming blue now permeates the interior of your abode. Before you know it, you'll forget what the proper postage is for the average mail bomb and think about doing things that are more personally fulfilling. These might include applying soothing hand lotions, burning aromatherapy candles, and watching *Oprah*.

The weather is no longer your own, and neither are the world's many problems. You're right where you've always wanted to be: By yourself, bathed in a wondrous hue of medium blue.

It doesn't get much better than this. At least not without cable.

TARP FAQ

WHAT'S THE PROPER WAY TO DISPOSE OF A BIG BLUE TARP? ARE BBTS RECYCLABLE?

A: **THIS IS A TOUGH ONE.** Tarps are, in fact, recyclable. They can be melted down and reused. But you might have trouble getting your local recycling center to take one. Try anyway. It's the least you can do. Otherwise, unfortunately, tarps go in the trash and wind up in landfills — likely their resting place for many, many hundreds of years, at the rate plastic decays.

Our preferred solution is more befitting the service the tarp has rendered, and infinitely more respectful: Remove it from its tethers, fold it neatly into a long strip, then again in triangular folds, much like you fold an old, tattered, revered flag. Store it in a place of honor in your garage or shed. For all it's done for you, you can give up a bit of shelf space. Besides, you never know when you might need to set up a windbreak.

Tarp Application 40

LOW-BUDGET POOL COVER/BODY BAG

WHERE:

Over the top of your $6.5 million swimming pool in the backyard of your $65 million Malibu weekend home or the $800,000 hot tub next to it

AS IF the BBT needed another special attribute to separate it from the flotsam of life, there's this: Tarps float.

Like a cork, really. Which is why you'll find them strewn on beaches from Malibu to Zanzibar, ostensibly after washing off or being dumped off ships.

You can harness that quality for the power of good by using a Big Blue Tarp as a replacement cover for the really expensive pool cover your next-door neighbor trashed when he belly flopped, in an inebriated state, into your pool at your last big Flag Day party.

It's pretty simple: Acquire a blue tarp in the size of your pool, or larger, trim it to fit, float it out there, and admire.

Secondary benefit: If your neighbor repeats his feat, just leave him there to flounder around on top of the tarp. When he stops moving, roll him up like pork in a burrito, pull the tarp out by one end, and drag him out to the curb.

We dare you to show us another common household product that can protect your investment in an aquatic exercise program *and* serve as a perfectly functional body bag.

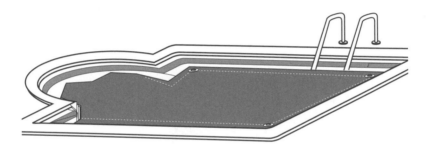

ABOUT THE AUTHOR

RON C. JUDD, the author of numerous best-selling outdoor guidebooks and a previous quasi-nonfiction work of humor, *The Roof Rack Chronicles*, is a twice-weekly columnist at the *Seattle Times*, the Northwest's leading newspaper *(www. seattletimes.com)*. His work has taken him around the globe, covering the Summer and Winter Olympics on four continents and the America's Cup in New Zealand, where he rode as a "17th man" in a sailboat race and, in spite of heavy seas, managed to not throw up. A Washington native and part-time journalism instructor, freelance writer, and photographer, he lives in Bellingham, Washington. Keep up with his work at *www.ronjudd.com*.